HOW TO BOIL
AN EGG . . .

W9-CHN-772

. . . and 156 other
simple recipes for one.

JAN ARKLESS

BOB ADAMS, INC.
PUBLISHERS
Holbrook, Massachusetts

Published by Bob Adams, Inc.
260 Center Street, Holbrook, MA 02343

ISBN: 1-55850-115-0

Printed in the United States of America

B   C   D   E   F   G   H   I   J

This publication is designed to provide accurate and authoritative information with regard to the subject matter covered. It is sold with the understanding that the publisher is not engaged in rendering legal, accounting, or other professional advice. If legal advice or other expert assistance is required, the services of a qualified professional person should be sought.
— From a *Declaration of Principles* jointly adopted by a Committee of the American Bar Association and a Committee of Publishers and Associations.

COVER PHOTO: Jay Brenner, FPG International

TABLE OF CONTENTS

VEGETABLES, VEGETABLE DISHES, AND RICE / 59

Globe artichokes; Jerusalem artichokes; Asparagus; Eggplant; Avocado; String beans; Bean sprouts; Broccoli; Brussels sprouts; Cabbage (white or green); Carrots; Cauliflower; Celeriac (celery root); Celery; Chicory; Chinese cabbage; Zucchini; Cucumber; Lettuce; Summer squash; Mushrooms; Okra; Onions; Parsnips; Peas; Peppers (green, red, or yellow); Potatoes (boiled); Potatoes (roast); Potatoes (new); Potatoes (sautéed); Potatoes (baked); Potatoes (baked stuffed); Potatoes (scalloped); Spinach; Rutabagas (swedes); Corn; Sweet potatoes and yams; Tomatoes; Turnips; Rice (boiled); Rice (fried); Risotto; Red cabbage; Basic green salad; Creamy avocado toast; Savory avocado snack; Stuffed peppers; Vegetable hot pot; Vegetable curry; Coleslaw; Crispy cabbage casserole.

BACON, SAUSAGE AND HAM / 121

Bacon; Sausages; A proper breakfast; Sausage and mashed potato; Braised sausages; Savory sausage meat pie; Toad in the hole; Sausage and bacon hubble bubble; Bacon-stuffed zucchini or squash; Farmhouse supper.

COOKED MEATS / 137

Fried liver and bacon with fried onions; Savory corned beef hash; Liver savory; Liver hot pot.

FISH / 143

Fried fish with butter; Fried or grilled trout (or mackerel); Cod steaks with cheese; Tomato fish bake; Tuna bake; Tuna fiesta; Cod in white wine.

BEEF / 151

Beef casserole or stew; Shepherd's pie; Potato bolognese;
Beef curry; Poppadums; Hamburgers; Beef stroganoff; Chili
con carne; Broiled (or pan-fried) steak; Kebabs.

CHICKEN / 169

Fried chicken; Chicken in tomato and mushroom sauce;
Chicken with corn—for 2; Roast chicken pieces; Easy
chicken casserole—for 2; Chicken curry; Hawaiian chicken;
Chicken in wine.

LAMB / 183

Lamb chops—broiled or fried; Oven chop; Irish stew; Lamb
stew.

PORK / 189

Pork chops—broiled or pan-fried; Mustard-glazed pork
chop; Pork chop in British cider or beer; Pork in a packet;
Crunchy fried pork; Spare ribs.

PASTA / 199

Macaroni and cheese; Bolognese sauce; Spaghetti bolognese; Spaghetti pork savory; Quick lasagna; Cheesy
noodles.

"SUNDAY LUNCH" DISHES / 209

Roast beef; Yorkshire pudding; Roast chicken; Roast leg or
shoulder of lamb; Roast pork; Gravy; White sauce; Onion
sauce; "Instant" sauce mix; Apple sauce; Mint sauce;
Stuffing.

Quick chocolate sauce—for ice cream; Hot chocolate sauce; Banana split; Fruit pavlova; Lemon meringue pie; Crêpes; Grilled peaches; Peaches with syrup; Liqueur oranges—for 2; Chocolate crunchies; Chocolate krispies.

INTRODUCTION

I originally wrote this book to help my son with his cooking when he went to college. I have since realized that the recipes contained here are useful not only for students but for people of all ages who find themselves alone and having to cook for themselves for the first time.

Other cook books assume some basic knowledge of cooking techniques. In this book I have assumed none. I wrote it specifically for people who know *absolutely nothing* or *very little* about cooking or meal planning.

The book explains the simple things we are supposed to know by instinct, such as how to boil an egg or fry sausages, or how to prepare and cook vegetables *and* have them ready to eat at the same time as the main course! It includes recipes and suggestions for a variety of snacks and main courses (not all cooked in the frying pan or made from ground beef) using fish, chicken, beef, lamb, and pork. The majority of the meals are quick, easy, and economical to make, but there is a "Sunday Lunch" chapter near the end of the book.

There are just a few recipes for desserts and cakes, which are easy to buy ready-made or frozen. Remember that yogurt makes a good, cheap dessert and that fresh fruit makes the best dessert of all. Also, fresh fruit juice or milk is far better for you than soft drinks or alcohol.

Most recipes in other cook books are geared towards feeding four or six people, but the recipes contained here are designed for the single person living on his or her own. However, this book does include a few recipes for two people. This is because it is easier to cook larger portions of stews and casseroles as very small helpings tend to dry up during cooking.

AMOUNTS TO USE WHEN COOKING FOR ONE

Pasta, noodles, shapes, etc.	— 1 very generous cup (3 oz.) uncooked pasta.
Potatoes	— 3–4 according to size.
Rice	— ⅓ cup dry uncooked rice.
Vegetables	— See individual vegetables in the vegetable chapter, page 59–119.
Oily fish	— 1 whole fish (trout, mackerel, herring).
White fish	— 6–8 oz. fillet cod, haddock, etc.
Roast beef	— Approximately 6 oz. per person. A roast weighing 2½–3 lbs. should serve 6–8 helpings; remember you can use cold meat for dinner next day.
Ground beef	— 4–6 oz.
Steak	— 6–8 oz. is a fair-sized steak.
Stewing beef	— 4–6 oz.
Lamb or pork chops	— 1 per person.
Roast lamb	— Because you are buying meat with a bone

in, you need to buy a larger roast to account for the bone. A roast weighing about 2½ lbs. will serve 4 people well.

Roast pork — Approximately 8 oz. per serving.

USING THE OVEN
Temperatures are given for both gas and electric ovens. Remember always to heat the oven for a few minutes before cooking food in it, so that the whole of the oven reaches the appropriate temperature.

One note of warning: *Food just reheated can make you extremely ill if not cooked through, especially pork and chicken—you have been warned!*

FOLLOWING THE RECIPES
I have given "preparation and cooking" times for the recipes in this book so that, before you start cooking, you will know approximately how much time to set aside for preparing and cooking the meal. The ingredients used in each recipe are listed in the order they are used in the directions. Collect all the specified ingredients *before* you start cooking, otherwise you may find yourself lacking a vital ingredient when you have already prepared half the meal. When the meal is ready, there should be no ingredients left—if there are, you have left something out!

ABBREVIATIONS AND MEASUREMENTS USED IN THE BOOK
The ingredients mentioned are all readily available. Meat, fish and vegetables can be weighed in the store when you buy them, or will have the weight on the package. Don't buy more than you need for the recipe; extras tend to get left at the back of the cupboard or refrigerator and wasted. But it is worthwhile buying some goods in larger quantities—rice,

pasta, ketchup, etc.—as they will keep fresh for a long time and be on hand when you need them.

In the recipes:
    tsp. = teaspoon
    tbsp. = tablespoon
    cup = 8 fluid oz.

Butter, margarine, etc.
    1-inch cube = 2 tbsp.

Cheese
    1-inch cube grated = ⅓ cup, approximately.

Sausages
    Breakfast — 8 sausages in an 8 oz. package.
    Thick sausages — 4 sausages in an 8 oz. package.

The following sections are particularly useful for students living away from home and cooking for themselves for the first time in their lives.

USEFUL SUPPLIES
Beg or borrow these from home or try to collect them at the beginning of the term, then just replace them during the year as necessary.

    Beef and chicken bullion cubes
    Coffee (instant)
    Coffee (real)
    Cooking oil
    Curry powder
    Dried mixed herbs

Flour
Garlic powder (or paste)
Gravy preparation mix of your choice
Horseradish sauce
Mustard
Non-dairy creamer (for coffee)
Pasta
Pepper
Relish
Rice (long grain)
Salt
Soy sauce
Sugar
Sweetened cocoa powder
Tabasco sauce
Tea bags
Tomato purée
Tomato sauce
Vinegar
Worcestershire sauce

ALSO
Dish towel, dishwashing liquid, abrasive sponge, oven cleaning powder.

Store sugar, rice, flour, pasta, and cookies in airtight containers rather than leaving them in open packages on the shelf. This keeps them fresh and clean for much longer and protects them from marauding insects. Try to collect some storage jars and plastic containers for this purpose (large, empty coffee jars with plastic lids, and plastic ice cream cartons are ideal).

PERISHABLE FOODS
These don't keep so long but are useful to have as a start.

Bacon
Cookies
Bread
Butter
Cereals (such as cornflakes)
Cheese
Eggs
Fruit juice
Frozen vegetables
Honey
Jam
Margarine
Milk
Peanut butter
Potatoes

HANDY CANS FOR A QUICK MEAL
Baked beans
Canned chili
Canned corn
Canned fruit
Canned soups
Canned tomatoes
Sardines
Soups—also dried soups
Spaghetti
Tuna fish
Vegetables (peas, carrots, etc.)

USEFUL KITCHEN EQUIPMENT
Aluminum foil
Bottle opener
Can opener

Casserole (thick heavy ones are the best)
Chopping/bread board
Cooking tongs
Dessert spoon
Frying pans — 2–3 different sizes; Teflon coated pans are easiest to use and clean
Grater
Kettle
Kitchen scissors
Knives — bread knife with serrated edge; sharp chopping knife for meat; vegetable knife
Oven-proof dish (Pyrex type)
Paper towels
Plastic wrap
Plastic storage containers (large ice cream tubs are useful to store cookies, pasta, etc.)
Saucepans — 1 small; 1 or 2 large ones
Set of measuring cups and spoons
Set of mixing bowls
Spatula
Storage jars (large empty coffee cans are ideal)
Wooden spoons

HANDY BUT NOT ESSENTIAL KITCHEN EQUIPMENT

Aluminum pans (these are cheap and last for several bakings; useful if you need a pan of a particular shape of size)
Baking pan (for meat)
Baking pans (various sizes)
Blender
Bread box
Colander
Egg whisk or egg beater

Mixer of food processor
Potato masher
Saucepans (extra) and/or casseroles
Sieve
Toaster

GLOSSARY

Various cooking terms used in the book (some of which may be unfamiliar to you) are explained in this glossary.

Al dente — referring to pasta that is cooked and feels firm when bitten.

Basting — spooning fat or butter or meat juices over food that is being roasted (particularly meat and poultry) to keep it moist.

Beating — mixing food with a wooden spoon or whisk so that the lumps disappear and it becomes smooth.

Binding — adding eggs, cream, or butter to a dry mixture to hold it together.

Blending — mixing dry ingredients (such as flour) with a little liquid to make a smooth, runny, lump-free mixture.

Boiling — cooking food in boiling water (i.e., at a temperate of 212°F) with the water bubbling gently.

Boning — removing the bones from meat, poultry or fish.

Braising — frying food in a hot fat so that it is browned, and then cooking it slowly in a covered dish with a little liquid and some vegetables.

Broiling — cooking food by direct heat under a broiler.

Casserole — an oven-proof dish with lid; also a slow-cooked stew.

Chilling — cooling food in a refrigerator without freezing.

Colander — a perforated metal or plastic basket used for straining food.

Deep-frying — immersing food in hot fat or oil and frying it.

Dicing — cutting food into small cubes.

Dot with butter — cover food with small pieces of butter.

Flaking — separating fish into flaky pieces.

Frying — cooking food in oil or fat in a pan (usually a flat frying pan).

Mixing — combining ingredients by stirring.

Next (making a) — arranging food (such as rice or potatoes) around the outside of a plate to make a circular border and putting other food into the middle of this "nest."

Poaching — cooking food in water that is just below boiling point.

Purée — food that has been passed through a sieve and reduced to pulp (or pulped in a blender or electric mixer).

Roasting — cooking food in a hot oven.

Sautéing — frying food quickly in hot, shallow fat, and turning it frequently in the pan so that is browns evenly.

Seasoning — adding salt, pepper, herbs, or spices to food.

Simmering — cooking food in water that is just below boiling point so that only an occasional bubble appears.

Straining — separating solid food from liquid by draining it through a sieve or colander (e.g., potatoes, peas, etc. that have been cooked in boiling water).

Eggs

Eggs are quick to cook and can make a nourishing snack or a main course in minutes. The first part of this chapter tells how to cook eggs simply, while the second part contains more sophisticated recipes.

BOILED EGG

Use an egg already at room temperature, not one straight from the refrigerator, since otherwise it may crack. Slip it carefully into a small saucepan, cover with warm (not boiling) water, and add a pinch of salt (to seal up any cracks). Bring to a boil, note the time, and turn down the heat before the egg starts rattling around in the pan. Simmer gently, timing from when the water begins to boil, using the table below:

Size	*Time*	*Description*
Large (sizes 1 or 2)	3 min.	soft-boiled
Standard (sizes 3 or 4)	2½ min.	soft-boiled
Large	4 min.	soft yolk and hard white
Standard	3½ min.	soft yolk and hard white
Large	10 min.	hard-boiled
Standard	9 min.	hard-boiled

SOFT-BOILED
Remove carefully from the pan with a spoon, put into an egg cup, and tap the top to crack the shell and prevent the egg from continuing to cook inside.

HARD-BOILED
Remove the pan from the heat and place under cold running water to prevent a black ring forming around the yolk. Peel off shell and rinse in cold water to remove any shell still clinging to the egg.

POACHED
EGG

Put about an inch of water into a clean frying pan and bring to a boil. Reduce the heat so that the water is just simmering. Crack the egg carefully into a cup and slide it into the simmering water. Cook very gently, just simmering in the hot water, for about 3 minutes until the egg is set to your liking. Lift it out with a slotted spoon or spatula, being careful not to break the yolk.

FRIED EGG

Heat a small amount of cooking oil, butter or drippings in a frying pan over a moderate heat (not too hot, or the egg white will disintegrate). Break egg into the frying pan and fry gently for 2 to 3 minutes. To cook the top of the egg, put the lid on the pan and let the heat cook it or carefully flip it over when half done. Remove the egg from the pan with a spatula.

SCRAMBLED
EGGS

Usually you will want to scramble 2 or more eggs at a time.

Chopped chives are tasty with scrambled eggs. Simply wash them, cut off their roots and chop them.

Beat the egg well with a fork or whisk in a bowl or large cup. Add salt, pepper, an ounce or two of milk, and chopped chives. Melt some butter (about a tbsp.) in a small, preferably heavy pan. Turn heat to low and pour in the beaten egg, stirring all the time, until the egg looks thick and creamy. Do not overcook because the egg will continue to cook even when removed from the heat.

CHEESY SCRAMBLED EGGS
Add ⅓ cup grated cheese to the beaten eggs before cooking.

PAN SCRAMBLE
If you are cooking sausages or bacon as well as scrambled eggs, fry the meat first and then cook the eggs in the same hot fat.

PIPERADE

Scrambled eggs plus a bit extra.

Preparation and cooking time: 30 minutes.

> **1 small onion**
> **Small green pepper**
> **2 tomatoes (fresh or canned)**
> **1 tbsp. oil or butter (for frying)**
> **Pinch of garlic powder**
> **Salt and pepper**
> **2–3 eggs**

Peel and slice the onion. Wash, core and chop the green pepper. Wash and chop the fresh tomatoes or drain the canned tomatoes and chop roughly. Heat the butter or oil in a saucepan and cook the onion and pepper over a medium heat, stirring well, until soft (about 5 minutes).

Add the chopped tomatoes, garlic, salt, and pepper and stir. Put a lid on the pan and continue to cook gently over a low heat, stirring occasionally, for about 15 to 20 minutes, to make a thick sauce.

Break the eggs into a small bowl or large cup. Lightly beat them with a fork, then pour them into the vegetable mixture, stirring hard with a wooden spoon, until the eggs are just setting. Pour onto a warm plate, and eat with hot buttered toast or crusty fresh bread rolls.

SAVORY
EGGS

A cheap and tasty variation on the bacon 'n egg theme; makes a good, quick supper.

Preparation and cooking time: 25 minutes.

> 1 small onion
> 1 small eating apple
> 1 strip uncooked bacon
> 1 tbsp. cooking oil or butter (for frying)
> Salt and pepper
> Sugar to taste
> 2 eggs

Peel and slice the onion. Wash, core and slice the apple. De-rind the bacon and cut into half-inch pieces. Heat the oil or butter in a frying pan over a moderate heat. Add the bacon, onion and apple, and fry, stirring occasionally until soft (about 5 minutes). Stir in the salt, pepper, and sugar.

Remove from the heat. Break the eggs into a cup, one at a time, and pour on top of the onion mixture. Cover the pan with a lid and cook for another 3 to 5 minutes over a very low heat until the eggs are as firm as you like them. For a change, cooked sliced sausages can be used instead of bacon.

BAKED EGG
WITH CHEESE

Quite delicious, and so easy to make.

Preparation and cooking time: 20 minutes.

> **1 to 1⅓ cups grated cheese**
> **2 eggs**
> **Salt and pepper**
> **1 tbsp. butter**

Heat the oven to 350°. Butter well an oven-proof dish. Cover the base of the dish with half the cheese. Break the eggs, one at a time, into a cup, then slide them carefully on top of the cheese. Season well with the salt and pepper and cover the eggs completely with the rest of the cheese.

Dot with the butter and bake in the hot oven for about 15 minutes, until the cheese is bubbling and the eggs are just set. Serve at once, with crusty French bread, rolls or crisp toast, or a salad.

EGG NESTS

These can be served plain or with the addition of grated cheese to make a very cheap lunch or supper.

Preparation and cooking time: 30 minutes.

> **2–4 potatoes**
> **1 tbsp. butter**
> **⅔ cups cheese (optional)**
> **Salt and pepper**
> **2 eggs**

Peel the potatoes, cut into thick slices and cook in boiling, salted water in a saucepan for 10 to 15 minutes, until soft. Drain and mash with a fork, then beat in the butter using a wooden spoon (see page 87). Grate the cheese, if used, and beat half of it into the potato. Season with the salt and pepper.

Grease an oven-proof dish. Spread the potato into this and make a nest for the eggs. Keep it warm. Boil and inch of water in a clean frying pan and poach the eggs (see page 19). If making cheesy eggs, heat the broiler. Carefully lift the eggs out of the water when cooked and put them into the potato nest. If making plain eggs, serve at once; otherwise cover the eggs with the remainder of the grated cheese and brown for a few moments under the broiler. Can be served with a fresh tomato or a salad.

SICILIAN
EGGS

Eggs and bacon with tomato sauce.

Preparation and cooking time: 25 minutes.

> **2 eggs**
> **1 small onion**
> **½ tbsp. butter**
> **1 8 oz. can of tomatoes**
> **Salt and pepper**
> **Pinch of sugar**
> **Pinch of dried herbs**
> **Strips of bacon (de-rinded)**

Hard-boil the eggs for 10 minutes (see page 18). Cool them in cold running water. Shell them, rinse clean, slice thickly and arrange in a greased, heat-proof dish. Peel and slice the onion and fry it in the butter in a small saucepan over a moderate heat until soft (about 5 minutes). Add the tomatoes, salt, pepper, sugar and herbs, and cook gently for another 5 minutes. Heat the broiler.

Pour the tomato mixture over the eggs, top with the de-rinded bacon strips, and place under the hot broiler until the bacon is cooked. If you do not have a broiler, fry the bacon in the pan with the onions, remove it and keep it hot while the tomatoes are cooking (see page 99), then top the tomato mixture with the hot, cooked bacon. Serve with toast.

EGG, CHEESE AND ONION SAVORY

Cheap and cheerful, eaten with chunks of hot, crusty bread.

Preparation and cooking time: 30 minutes.

> **2 eggs**
> **1 onion**
> **1 tbsp. butter (for frying)**

For the cheese sauce (you can omit this and just use grated cheese or a packaged sauce mix):
> **⅓ cup grated cheese**
> **1 tbsp. flour**
> **1 cup milk**
> **1 tbsp. butter**
> **Salt and pepper**
> **Pinch of mustard**

Hard boil the eggs for 10 minutes (see page 18). Peel and slice the onion and fry gently in the butter in a small saucepan over a moderate heat, for 4 to 5 minutes, until soft and cooked.

For the cheese sauce:
Mix the flour into a smooth paste with a little of the milk in a small bowl. Heat the rest of the milk to just short of boil-

ing and pour onto the flour mixture, stirring all the time. Then pour the whole mixture back into the saucepan and stir over the heat until the mixture thickens. Stir in the butter and beat well. Add the grated cheese, salt, pepper, and mustard.

Put the onion into a greased oven-proof dish. Slice the cold, peeled, hard-boiled eggs and arrange on top of the onion. Cover with the cheese sauce and sprinkle with the rest of the grated cheese. Brown under a hot broiler for a few minutes until the cheese is melted, crisp, and bubbly.

MURPHY'S
EGGS

A cheap and filling supper dish if you have time to wait for it to cook in the oven.

Preparation and cooking time: 1 hour, 15 minutes.

> **3–4 potatoes according to appetite**
> **1 onion**
> **1 strip of bacon**
> **Salt and pepper**
> **⅓–⅔ cup hot milk**
> **1 tsp. butter**
> **2 eggs**

Peel the potatoes, cut into half-inch cubes. Peel and slice the onion. De-rind and chop the bacon. Grease an oven-proof dish. Mix the potatoes, onion, and bacon in a bowl and put into the dish, seasoning well with the salt and pepper. Add the hot milk (enough to come halfway up the dish) and dot with the butter.

Bake at 400°, covered with a lid or foil for 45 minutes to an hour until the potatoes are cooked and all the milk is absorbed. Break each egg into a cup. Remove the dish of potatoes from the oven, make two hollows in the top of the potatoes with a spoon, and slip the raw eggs into the hollows. Return the dish to the oven for 6 to 8 minutes until the eggs are set. Serve at once.

FRENCH
TOAST

A boarding school favorite.

Preparation and cooking time: 15 minutes.

> **1 egg**
> **Sugar to taste**
> **⅓ cup milk**
> **3–4 thick slice white bread**
> **1 tbsp. butter (for frying)**

Serve with maple syrup, honey or jam, or sprinkled with white or brown sugar, or make it savory and sprinkle with salt, pepper, and a blob of tomato sauce.

Break the egg into a bowl or a large cup, add the sugar, and beat well with a whisk, mixer, or fork, gradually adding the milk. Pour this egg mixture into a shallow dish or soup plate and soak each slice of bread in the egg until it is all soaked up.

Heat a frying pan over a moderate heat. Melt the butter in the pan and fry the soaked bread slices in the hot butter, turning to cook both sides until golden brown and crispy. Serve at once, sprinkled with sugar (or salt, pepper or tomato sauce), or dripping with syrup, hone or jam. Savory french toast goes well with bacon, sausages, and baked beans.

FRENCH
OMELET

The best-known type of omelet: light golden egg, folded over into an envelope shape. Served plain or with a wide variety fillings folded inside. There is no need for a special omelet pan, unless you happen to own one, of course. Use any clean, ordinary frying pan.

Preparation and cooking time: 10 minutes.

> **2–3 eggs**
> **1 tsp. cold water per egg**
> **Pinch of salt and pepper (omit for sweet omelets)**
> **1 tsp. butter**
> **Filling as required (see below)**

Prepare the filling (see list on page 32). Warm a plate. Break the eggs into a bowl or large cup, add the water, salt, and pepper and beat with a fork.

Put the butter in a frying pan and heat over a moderate heat until it is just sizzling (but not brown). Place the egg mixture in the pan at once. Tilt the pan in all directions so that the uncooked egg in the middle can run onto the hot pan and set. Continue until all the egg is very lightly cooked underneath and the top is still running and soft (about one minute). The top will cook in its own heat when it is folded over.

With a spatula, loosen the omelet so that you can remove it easily from the pan. Put the filling across the middle of it and fold both sides over to make an envelope. If using a cold filling, cook for a further minute. Remove from the pan and place on the warm plate. Serve at once with French bread, rolls, potatoes, a side salad, or just a fresh tomato. Delicious!

OMELET FILLINGS

SAVORY

Fresh or dried herbs	— Add 1 tsp. chopped herbs to the beaten eggs, water and seasoning.
Grated cheese	— ⅓ to ⅔ cups
Cooked meat	— Chop 1–2 slices cooked ham or sausages.
Mushrooms	— Wash and chop 2 oz. (4–5 mushrooms). Cook gently in a small pan with a tsp. of butter for 2–3 minutes, stirring occasionally. Keep hot.
Bacon	Fry 1–2 strips of bacon in a little oil or fat (see page 122). Keep hot.
Tomato	— Wash 1–2 tomatoes, slice and fry them in a little oil or fat, and keep hot. Or slice a washed tomato and use raw.
Chicken	— 2–3 tbsp. chopped, cooked chicken. (You can use the pickings from a roast chicken.)
Asparagus	— 5 oz. canned asparagus tips. Heat them through in a small saucepan. Drain and keep hot.

SWEET

Jam	— Warm 1–2 tbsp. jam by placing in a small dish and standing in a saucepan with 2 inches of hot water, warming gently over a low heat.

Fruit	— Add 2–3 tbsp. sliced, canned fruit (peaches, pineapple or apricot)
or	Use 2–3 tbsp. sliced fresh fruit (bananas, peaches, strawberries, or raspberries).
Marmalade	— Add 2–3 tbsp. orange or ginger marmalade.
Honey	— Add 2–3 tbsp. honey.
Honey & walnut	— Use 2–3 tbsp. honey, 1 tbsp. chopped walnuts.
Chocolate	— Sprinkle 2 tbsp. sweetened cocoa powder over the omelet, dot with butter, and fold over carefully.

Sprinkle sweet omelets with 1 tsp. powdered or granulated sugar just before serving.

SPANISH
OMELET

A delicious, filling, savory omelet. Served flat like a thick pancake, mixed with onion, potato, cooked meat, and other vegetables—a good way of using up cold cooked left-overs. (A large omelet, made with 4 eggs and some extra vegetables, can be cut in half, serving 2 people.)

Preparation and cooking time: 15 minutes.

EXTRAS (optional):

Cooked meat — 1–2 slices chopped, cooked ham or sausages

Bacon — 1–2 strips of bacon, chopped and fried with the onion.

Vegetables — 1–2 tbsp. cold cooked vegetables (peas, corn, green beans, mixed vegetables).

Green peppers — 1–2 tbsp. green peppers, chopped and mixed with the onion.

   1 small onion
   2–3 boiled potatoes
   2–3 eggs
   1 tsp. cold water per egg
   Salt and pepper
   Pinch of dried herbs (optional)
   1 tbsp. oil (for frying)

Prepare the "extras," if used. Peel and chop the onion.

Dice the cooked potatoes (see page 87). Beat the eggs, water, salt and pepper and herbs lightly with a fork in a small bowl.

Heat the oil in an omelet or frying pan over a medium heat and fry the onion for 3 to 5 minutes until soft. Add the diced potato and continue frying until the potato is thoroughly heated. Add the extra meat or vegetables (if used) and heat through again. Heat the broiler and warm a plate. Pour the beaten egg mixture into the pan over the vegetables, and cook without stirring until the bottom is firm but the top still creamy and moist (about 1 to 2 minutes). Shake the pan occasionally to prevent sticking.

Place under the hot broiler for half a minute until the top is set—beware in case the pan handle gets hot. Slide the omelet flat onto the warm plate and serve at once.

QUICK
EGG AND
VEGETABLE
CURRY

A fast and easy curry recipe.

Preparation and cooking time: 35 minutes.

> **1 onion**
> **1 tsp. butter**
> **1 tsp. cooking oil**
> **1 tsp. curry powder (or to taste)**
> **1 tsp. flour**
> **10 oz. can mulligatawny soup**
> **2 eggs**
> **⅓ cup long grain rice**
> **1 cup frozen mixed vegetables**

Peel and chop the onion, and fry in the oil and butter in a saucepan over a medium heat, until soft (about 3 to 4 minutes). Stir in the curry powder and flour and cook very gently for another 2 minutes, stirring all the time. Gradually stir in the soup, bring to the boil, reduce the heat to a simmer, put on the lid, and cook gently for about 20 minutes, stirring occasionally, to make a thick sauce.

Hard-boil the eggs for 10 minutes (see page 18). Rinse them under cold, running water, peel them, wash off the shell, and cut in half, lengthways. Cook the rice for 10 to 12 minutes in a large pan of boiling salted water (see page 101). Drain and keep hot, fluffing with a fork to keep it from getting lumpy. Add the mixed vegetables to the curry sauce and bring back to a boil

Put the rice onto a warm plate, spreading with a spoon to form a ring. Arrange the eggs in the center and cover with the vegetable curry sauce. Serve with any side dishes you like (see page 158).

EGG NOG

A nourishing breakfast for those in a hurry, or an easily-digested meal for those feeling fragile!

Preparation time: 5 minutes.

> 1 egg
> 2 tsp. sugar
> 1¼ cups milk, cold or warm
> 2 tsp. brandy, rum, or whiskey (optional, but not
>   for breakfast!)
> or
> 1 tbsp. sherry (again, not for breakfast)
> Pinch of nutmeg or cinnamon

Break the egg into a bowl and beat it lightly with a mixer, egg whisk, or fork, adding the sugar and gradually beating in the milk. Add the spirits (if used). Pour into a tall glass, sprinkle nutmeg or cinnamon on top, and serve at once.

HOW TO SEPARATE AN EGG

METHOD 1
Have ready 2 cups or bowls. Crack the egg carefully and pull
the 2 halves of the shell slightly apart, letting the white drain
into one bowl and keeping the yolk in the shell until all the
white has drained out. Tip the yolk into the other bowl. If the
yolk breaks, tip the whole thing into a third bowl and start
again with another egg.

METHOD 2
Carefully break the egg and tip it onto a saucer, making sure
the yolk is not broken. Place a glass over the yolk and gently
tip the white into a bowl, keeping the yolk on the saucer with
the glass.

METHOD 3
Use an egg separator, available from stores. Place the
separator over a cup and crack the egg into its concave center.

CHEESE

Here are some delicious snacks using cheese—they're simple and quick to make.

EASY WELSH RAREBIT (CHEESE ON TOAST)

This is the quickest method of making cheese on toast. It can be served plain or topped with relish, sliced tomato, or crispy, cooked bacon.

Preparation and cooking time: 5–10 minutes.

> 1–3 strips of bacon (optional)
> 1–2 tomatoes (optional)
> 2–3 slices cheese
> 2–3 slices of bread (white or brown)
> 1 tbsp. relish (optional)

Heat the broiler. Lightly broil the bacon, if used (see page 122). Slice the tomatoes, if used. Slice the cheese, making enough slices to cover the pieces of bread. Toast the bread lightly on both sides. Arrange the slices of cheese on one side of the toast and put under the broiler for 1 to 2 minutes, until the cheese begins to bubble. Top with the tomato slices, bacon, or relish and return to the broiler for another minute, to heat the topping and brown the cheese. Eat at once.

TRADITIONAL
WELSH
RAREBIT

More soft and creamy than cheese on toast, and only takes a few more minutes to prepare.

Preparation and cooking time: 10 minutes.

> **1–3 strips of bacon (optional)**
> **1–2 tomatoes (optional**
> **⅔-1 cup of grated cheese**
> **1 tsp. milk**
> **Pinch of mustard**
> **Shake of pepper**
> **1 tbsp. relish (optional)**
> **2–3 slices of bread**

Heat the broiler. Lightly broil the bacon, if used (see page 122). Slice the tomatoes, if used. Mix the cheese into a stiff paste with the milk in a bowl, stirring in the mustard and pepper. Lightly toast the bread and generously cover it with the cheese mixture. Put under the hot broiler for 1 to 2 minutes, until the cheese starts to bubble. Top with the bacon, tomato slices or pickle, and return to the broiler for another minute, to heat the topping and brown the cheese. Serve at once.

BUCK
RAREBIT

Welsh Rarebit with poached eggs. When the toast is covered with cheese and ready to go back under the broiler to brown, prepare 1 or 2 poached eggs, by cooking them gently in simmering water for 2 to 3 minutes (see page 19). While the eggs are cooking, put the toast and cheese slices under the grill to brown. When they are golden and bubbling and the eggs are cooked, carefully remove the eggs from the water and slide them onto the hot toast and cheese. Serve immediately.

WELSH
RAREBIT
WITH BEER

Open a can of beer, use a little in the cooking, and drink the rest with your meal.

Preparation and cooking time: 10–15 minutes.

⅔-1 cup grated cheese
Butter
1–2 tbsp. beer
Shake of pepper
Pinch of mustard
1–2 slices of bread (white or brown)

Heat the broiler. Melt the butter in a small saucepan over a moderate heat. Add the cheese, beer, pepper, and mustard and stir well over the heat until the cheese begins to melt and the mixture to boil. Remove the saucepan from the heat. Toast the bread lightly on both sides. Carefully pour the cheese mixture onto the toast and put back under the broiler for a few moments until the cheese is hot, bubbling, and golden brown. Serve at once; delicious!

HOT DOG
AND CHEESE
ON TOAST

A quick snack made with food from the cupboard.

Preparation and cooking time: 15 minutes.

> **2–3 slices of bread**
> **2–3 slices of cooked ham or sausage (optional)**
> **Approximately 4 hot dogs**
> **2–3 slices of cheese (pre-packed slices are ideal)**

Heat the broiler. Lightly toast the bread on one side. Lay the ham or sausage on the untoasted side and top with the hot dogs. Cover with the cheese slices and cook under the hot broiler until the cheese has melted. Eat at once.

If you don't have a broiler the bread can be heated in a 400° oven for a few minutes. Place the "toast" with the topping back into the oven, on an oven-proof dish, and cook for 5 to 10 minutes until the cheese has melted.

CAULIFLOWER
CHEESE

Filling enough for a supper dish with crusty French bread and butter; or serve as a vegetable dish with meat or fish.

Preparation and cooking time: 30 minutes.

> **1 portion (3–4 florets) cauliflower**
> **1 slice of bread (crumbled or grated into crumbs)**
> **1 tsp. of butter**
> **1 sliced tomato (optional)**

For the cheese sauce (alternatively, use packaged sauce mix or grated cheese alone):

> **⅔ cup grated cheese**
> **1 tbsp. flour**
> **1 cup milk**
> **1 tbsp. butter or margarine**
> **Salt and pepper**
> **Pinch of mustard**

Trim the cauliflower's stalk, divide it into florets, and wash thoroughly. Cook it in boiling, salted water for 5 minutes until just tender. Drain well. Make the cheese sauce. Put the cauliflower into a greased oven-proof dish. Cover with the cheese sauce, sprinkle the breadcrumbs on top and a tsp. of butter, and add the tomato slices. Place under a hot broiler for a few minutes until golden-brown and crispy. (If you do not have time to make the cheese sauce, cover the cauliflower with ⅔ cup grated cheese and broil as above.)

SNACKS AND SAVORIES

Just a few ideas and suggestions for quick snacks and packed lunches. Other recipes can be found in the egg and cheese chapters'

BEANS (OR SPAGHETTI) ON TOAST

Just in case you've never cooked these before, here is how you do it.

Preparation and cooking time: 5 minutes.

> ⅓ cup grated cheese (optional)
> **1 8 oz. can of beans, spaghetti, spaghetti-o's, etc.**
> **2–3 slices of bread**
> **Butter**

Put the beans or spaghetti into a small saucepan and heat slowly over a moderate heat, stirring occasionally. Toast the bread. When the beans are beginning to bubble, stir gently until they are thoroughly heated. Put the toast onto a warm plate, and pour the beans on top of the buttered side (some people prefer the toast left at the side of the plate). Sprinkle the cheese on top. Eat at once.

SANDWICHES
FOR PACKED
LUNCHES

Use different kinds of bread for variety—white, brown, crusty rolls, French bread, and pita bread are a few suggestions. Spread the bread lightly with butter or mayo; this keeps it from getting soggy if the filling is moist and holds the filling in place (have you ever tried eating dry egg sandwiches?). Wrap the sandwiches in plastic wrap to keep them fresh—it's worth buying a roll if you take sandwiches often—or put them into a plastic bag. A plastic container will keep them from getting squashed.

Lettuce, tomato, cucumber, celery, and green peppers are a good addition, either sliced in the sandwiches or eaten separately. Treat yourself to some fresh fruit, too, according to what is in season.

Cheese	— Slice or grate the cheese.
Cheese and relish	— Slice or grate the cheese and mix with a little relish or chutney.
Cheese slices	— Quick and easy. Use straight from the package. Spread relish on top of the cheese, if liked.
Cheese and tomato	— Slice a tomato layer on top of the cheese.
Cheese and onion	— Peel and thinly slice an onion, lay it thinly on top of the sliced cheese.

Cold meat	— Sliced, cooked meat, from the supermarket or delicatessen—ham, bologna, turkey, chicken, salami, etc. Buy according to your taste and pocket. Buy fresh as you need it; do not store too long in the refrigerator.

Cold meat from the Sunday roast:

Beef and mustard or horseradish sauce	— Slice the beef thinly and spread with the mustard or horseradish.
Cold lamb and mint sauce	— Slice the meat, cut off any excess fat. Sprinkle with the mint sauce.
Cold pork and apple sauce and stuffing	— Slice the pork, spread with the apple sauce and stuffing, if you have any left.
Cold chicken	— Use up the scraps from a roast chicken or buy sliced chicken from the deli. Spread with cranberry sauce and stuffing. Do not store for too long in the refrigerator; buy just a little at a time.
Egg	— Cook for 10 minutes in boiling water (see page 18). Shell, wash and mash with a fork. Mix it with a little mayonnaise. One egg will fill two sandwiches.
Peanut butter	— No need to butter the bread first. Jelly optional.
Salad	— Washed lettuce, sliced tomato, sliced

cucumber, layered together.

Tuna fish — Open a can, drain off the oil or water. Tip the tuna fish into a bowl and mash with mayonnaise. Spread on bread and top with lettuce.

Liver pâté — Choose from the numerous smooth or rough pâtés in the supermarket. Brown bread is particularly good with pâté.

Eat with your packed lunch:

Cottage cheese (plain or flavored) — Eat from the carton with a fresh buttered roll or an apple. Don't forget to take a spoon.

Yogurt — Eat from the carton—remember to take a spoon.

Hard-boiled egg — Shell and wash it. Pop it into a plastic bag and eat with a fresh buttered roll.

GRILLED
CHEESE
SANDWICH

Preparation and cooking time: 10 minutes.

For each sandwich, use the following:

> **2 slices of bread**
> **Butter**
> **Enough thinly-sliced cheese to cover one side of
> bread**

Preheat broiler. Butter both slices of bread on one side and lay cheese in between slices, butter side out. With a spatula, place sandwich on rack under broiler, turning when it becomes golden brown. Remove when both sides are toasted and cheese is melted.

Extra fillings (optional):
Place these in sandwich before broiling.
> Thin slices of tomato
> Tuna fish
> Sliced ham or cooked bacon

GARLIC
BREAD

A sophisticated alternative to hot rolls.

Preparation and cooking time: 18–20 minutes.

> **1 garlic clove (or ½ tsp. garlic powder or paste)**
> **2 tbsp. butter**
> **½ French loaf or 1–2 bread rolls (according to appetite)**
> **Large piece of cooking foil (for wrapping)**

Peel, chop and crush the garlic clove, if used, until smooth. (You can crush it with a pestle and mortar or garlic press, if you have one, or use the flat side of a knife.) Cream together the butter and crushed garlic (or garlic powder or paste), until soft and well-mixed.

Cut the loaf nearly through into one-inch slices or cut the rolls in half. Butter the slices of the loaf, or the rolls, generously on both sides with the garlic butter and press the loaf or rolls together again. Wrap the loaf or rolls loosely in the foil. Heat the bread in a 400° oven until hot and crisp (approximately 5 minutes). Serve at once, with the foil unfolded.

GARLIC
MUSHROOMS

Delicious, but don't breathe over other people after eating it!
Serve with fried bacon to make a more substantial meal.

Preparation and cooking time: 10 minutes.

> **¼ lb. mushrooms**
> **1 clove fresh garlic (or garlic powder or garlic**
>   **paste)**
> **½ strips of bacon (optional)**
> **2 tbsp. butter with 1 tsp. cooking oil**
> **2 thick slices of bread**

Wash the mushrooms. Peel, chop, and crush the fresh
garlic, if used. Fry the bacon and keep hot (see page 122).
Melt the butter and oil in a saucepan over a moderate heat.
Add the garlic (fresh, powder, or paste) and mushrooms.

Stir well and fry gently for 3 to 5 minutes, stirring and
spooning the garlic-flavored butter over the mushrooms.
While the mushrooms are cooking, toast the bread lightly, cut
in half, and put onto a hot plate. Spoon the mushrooms onto
the toast and pour the remaining garlic butter over the top.
Top with bacon, if used. Eat at once.

PIZZA

There are so many makes, shapes and sizes of pizzas available now, both fresh and frozen, that it hardly seems worth the effort of making your own. However, these commercial ones are usually improved by adding your own extras during the cooking, either when under the grill or in the oven according to the instructions on the package.

Add these extras for the last 5 to 10 minutes of cooking time by spreading them on top of the pizza:

Cheese	— Use grated or thinly sliced.
Ham	— Chop and sprinkle over the pizza.
Salami or sausage	— Chop or fold slices and arrange on top of the pizza.
Mushrooms	— Wash and slice thinly, spread over the pizza.
Tomatoes	— Slice thinly, spread over the pizza.
Olives	— A few spread on top add color and flavor.
Anchovies	— Arrange crisscross over the pizza.

VEGETABLES, VEGETABLE DISHES, AND RICE

To preserve flavor and nutrients during cooking, vegetables are best steamed rather than boiled. A small steamer can be purchased separately, or you can buy a large pot and steamer set. Such a set can be used in a variety of tasks and will well repay the cost of purchase.

To steam, fill the bottom of the pot with water up to the perforations in the steamer and bring to a boil. Add vegetables, reduce heat, and cover. Vegetables are best left slightly crisp, so check frequently and do not overcook. Take care not to let all the water in the pot boil away during cooking, or the bottom of the pan may burn.

The water left over after steaming is rich with valuable nutrients and can be used in soups and gravies, if desired.

GLOBE
ARTICHOKES

Artichokes look large, but as you only eat the bottom tip of each leaf, you do need *a whole artichoke for each person.*

Cut off the stem of the artichoke to make the base level, snip off the points of the leaves (optional), and wash the artichoke well in cold water. Place in a steamer over boiling salted water and cook for 45 minutes, or until a leaf will pull off easily.

Drain the water from the pan and then turn the artichoke upside down in the pan for a few moments to drain any remaining water. Serve with plenty of butter. If you have never eaten an artichoke before, cook an extra one for a friend to show you how.

JERUSALEM
ARTICHOKES

Unrelated to the globe variety of artichokes, Jerusalem artichokes, which are the tubers of sunflowers, look like knobby potatoes. Cook them as soon as they are peeled, as they go brown very quickly even in cold water. A little lemon juice in the cooking water helps to keep them white. *8 oz. serves 1–2 portions.*

STEAMED OR BOILED
Peel and cut into evenly-sized lumps about the size of small potatoes. Steam or boil for 20 to 30 minutes or until tender. Drain and serve with a dab of butter.

STEAMED OR BOILED WITH CHICKEN SAUCE
Cook as above. Drain and put back in the saucepan with ½ cup condensed chicken soup. Bring to a boil, stirring occasionally. Tip the artichokes onto a warm plate and pour the chicken sauce over them.

SAUTÉED
Peel the artichokes and cut them into thick slices or chunks. Put 1 tsp. cooking oil and 1 tbsp. butter into a frying pan, add the artichoke pieces, and cook gently, turning frequently, for 15 to 20 minutes until soft. Tip the artichokes onto a warm plate and pour the buttery sauce over them.

ASPARAGUS

Usually sold in bundles, enough for 2–4 servings.

Snap off the woody ends of the stems and then scrape off the white tough parts. Rinse. Tie the stems into a bundle with clean string or white cotton and stand them upright in a steamer or in a tall pan with the stems in 1 inch of boiling water. Cover the pan and boil for 8 to 10 minutes until tender. Remove them carefully from the pan. Asparagus can be eaten with melted butter.

EGGPLANT

These lovely, shiny, purple-skinned vegetables are best left unpeeled.

Allow ½ lb. eggplant per person.

To get rid of any bitter taste before cooking, slice the eggplant into half-inch pieces. Put into a colander or strainer (if you do not have one, lay the slices on a piece of kitchen paper), sprinkle with salt, press a heavy plate down on top and leave for 30 minutes so that the bitter juices are pressed out. Wash and dry the slices. Heat a little oil in a frying pan and sauté gently until soft (about 5 minutes).

AVOCADO

Choose avocados that yield slightly when pressed gently. Unripe avocados feel very hard.

Slice the avocado in half lengthways, cutting through to the pit. Then separate the two halves by twisting gently. Remove the pit with the tip of the knife, trying not to damage the flesh, which should be soft and buttery in texture.

Cut avocados discolor very quickly, so prepare them just before serving or rub the cut halves with lemon juice to keep them from going brown. Serve avocados plain with a squeeze of lemon juice, with a vinaigrette dressing, or with any of numerous fillings spooned into the cavity where the stone was removed. Brown bread and butter is a good accompaniment, with a garnish of lettuce, tomato, and cucumber.

See page 109 for Creamy Avocado Toast and page 110 for Savory Avocado Snack.

SOME FILLING IDEAS

Vinaigrette — Mix well 2 tsp. oil, 1 tsp. vinegar, salt, pepper and a pinch of sugar.

Mayonnaise — 1 tbsp. mayonnaise.

Cottage cheese — Use 2 tbsp. cottage cheese (plain or with chives, pineapple, etc.).

Prawn or shrimp — Mix gently together 1–2 tbsp. shelled prawns or shrimp (fresh or frozen), 1 tbsp. mayonnaise or cottage cheese. A sauce can also be made with a mixture of 1 tbsp. salad dressing and a dash of ketchup.

Egg — Shell and chop 1 hard-boiled egg (see

page 18). Mix gently with 1 tbsp. mayonnaise or cottage cheese.

Yogurt — 2 tbsp. yogurt on its own or mixed with a chopped tomato and a few slices chopped cucumber.

STRING
BEANS

Allow approximately ¼ lb. per serving.

Cut off the ends of the beans with a vegetable knife or a pair of scissors. Wash beans and cut the longer ones in half. Put them into a steamer or a pan of boiling, salted water and cook for 2 to 5 minutes until just tender. Drain well and serve them with butter.

FROZEN WHOLE STRING BEANS
Allow approximately 3–4 oz. per serving. Cook in boiling, salted water as directed on the package and serve with butter. Very tasty, but be careful not to overcook them.

BEAN
SPROUTS

These can be cooked on their own but are better when cooked with a mixture of stir-fried vegetables.

Allow ¼ lb. per portion.

Soak for 10 minutes in cold water, then drain well. Heat 1 tbsp. oil in a frying pan or a wok, add the beansprouts and fry for 1 to 2 minutes, stirring all the time. Serve at once.

BROCCOLI

Allow 2–3 pieces or ½ lb. per serving.

Remove any coarse outer leaves and cut off the ends of the stalks. Wash well in cold water. Broccoli may be cut up or cooked whole in a steamer or upright in an inch of boiling water until tender. Serve with butter and/or lemon juice.

FROZEN BROCCOLI
Allow 4–6 oz. per serving, according to appetite. Cook as directed on the package.

BRUSSELS
SPROUTS

Try to buy firm, green sprouts of approximately the same size. Yellow outside leaves are a sign of old age.

Allow 4–6 oz. per serving.

Cut off the stalk ends and trim off the outer leaves, if necessary. Wash well. Steam for 5 to 10 minutes until tender. Serve with butter.

FROZEN SPROUTS
Allow 3–4 oz. per serving. Cook as directed on the package.

WHITE OR GREEN CABBAGE

(For red cabbage, see page 106.)

A much-maligned vegetable, evoking memories of school days. If cooked properly, cabbage is really delicious, and it's much cheaper than a lot of other vegetables. Cabbage goes a long way, so either buy *a small cabbage* and use it for several meals (cooked, or raw in a winter salad) or *just buy half or a quarter of a cabbage*.

Trim off the outer leaves and the stalk. Cut into quarters and shred, not too finely, removing the central core and cutting that into small pieces. Wash the cabbage. Boil it in an inch of salted water for 2 to 5 minutes. Do not overcook. Drain well, serve with butter or with a cheese sauce (see the recipe for cauliflower with cheese, page 47). For other recipes using cabbage as a main ingredient, see pages 117 and 118.

WINTER SALAD

Trim, shred and wash the cabbage. Drain well and dry in a salad shaker (if you have one) or put into a clean dish towel and shake or pat dry. Put the cabbage in a dish with any other salad vegetables, such as raw, grated carrot, tomato quarters, cucumber, celery, peppers, and peeled sliced onion. It can be served either on its own or with a dressing made from the following ingredients mixed together thoroughly: 4 tsp. salad oil, 2 tsp. vinegar, and a pinch of salt, pepper, and sugar.

CARROTS

New carrots can simply be scrubbed and cooked whole, like new potatoes. Older, larger carrots should be scraped or peeled, then cut in halves, quarters, slices, rings or dice, as preferred. The smaller the pieces, the quicker the carrots will cook.

Allow ¼ lb. per serving.

Scrub, peel and slice the carrots as necessary. Steam them or boil in half an inch of salted water for 5 to 20 minutes, according to their size, until just tender. Serve with butter.

BUTTERED CARROTS

Prepare the carrots as above, leaving tender, young carrots whole or slicing old carrots into rings. Place in a saucepan with ⅓ cup water, 1 tbsp. butter, 1 tsp. sugar, and a pinch of salt. Bring to a boil, then reduce the heat and simmer for 10 to 20 minutes until the carrots are tender. Take the lid off the saucepan, turn up the heat for a few minutes, and let the liquid bubble away until only a little sauce is left. Put the carrots onto a plate and pour the sauce over them.

FROZEN CARROTS OR MIXED VEGETABLES

Allow 3–4 oz. per serving. Cook as directed on the package and serve as above.

CAULIFLOWER

Most cauliflowers are too large for one person, but they can be cut in half and the remainder kept in the refrigerator for use in the next few days. Try not to bruise the florets when cutting them, as they will discolor easily. Very small cauliflower and packets of cauliflower florets are sold in some supermarkets. Allow 3–4 florets per serving.

Trim off tough stem and outer leaves. The cauliflower can be either left whole or divided into florets. Wash thoroughly. Steam or cook upright in an inch of boiling, salted water for 5 to 15 minutes, according to size, until just tender. Drain well. Serve hot with butter, a spoonful of sour cream, or white sauce (see page 221). For cauliflower with cheese, see page 47.

FROZEN CAULIFLOWER
Allow 4–6 oz. per serving. Cook as directed on the package and serve as above.

CELERIAC
(Celery
Root)

The root of a variety of celery, celeriac is one of the more unusual vegetables now available in good supermarkets.

Allow 4–8 oz. per person.

Peel fairly thickly and cut into evenly-sized chunks. Steam, or cover with boiling water and cook for 30 to 40 minutes or until tender. Serve with butter or mash with a potato masher, fork, or whisk with a little butter and milk. Season with salt and pepper.

CELERY

Most popular eaten raw, with cream cheese or peanut butter or chopped up in a salad. It can be cooked and served as a hot vegetable; the tougher outer stems can be used for cooking, leaving the tender inner stems to be eaten raw.

Allow ½ cup of celery per serving.

Chop the celery into 1-inch lengths. Steam, or drop gradually into ½ inch of boiling, salted water. Cook for about 10 minutes, until just tender. Serve with butter, or put into a greased, oven-proof dish, top with grated cheese, and brown under the broiler.

CHICORY

This can be used raw in salads or cooked carefully in water and butter, and served hot.

Allow 6–8 oz. per serving.

Remove any damaged outer leaves and trim the stalk. With a pointed vegetable knife, cut a cone-shaped core out of the base, to ensure even cooking and reduce bitterness. Wash in cold water. Put the chicory into a saucepan with butter, 2–3 tbsp. water, and a pinch of salt. Cook gently for about 20 minutes, until just tender, making sure that all the liquid does not disappear. Serve with melted butter.

CHINESE
CABBAGE

These can be used raw in salads. Keep the Chinese leaves in a plastic bag in the refrigerator to keep them crisp until you want to use them.

Allow ¼–½ small cabbage per serving.

Trim off any spoiled leaves and stalks. Shred finely. Wash and drain well (in a salad spinner or a clean dish towel). Use in salad with any other salad vegetables (cucumber, tomato, cress, spring onions, radish, etc.) and a vinaigrette dressing (see page 64).

ZUCCHINI

Allow 1 or 2 zucchini (4–6 oz.) per serving.

Cut the ends off very tiny zucchini and leave them whole. Cut larger ones into thin slices or ½ inch cubes. Wash well.

STEAMED OR BOILED

Steam, or boil gently in ½ inch salted water for 2 to 5 minutes until just tender. Drain them very well, as they tend to be a bit watery. (You can get them really dry by shaking them in the pan over a very low heat for a moment.) Serve with butter or tip them into a greased, oven-proof dish, top with grated cheese, and brown under a hot broiler. Zucchini can also be served with white, cheese, or parsley sauce (see page 221).

SAUTÉED

Prepare the zucchini as above. Wash and drain them well and dry on kitchen paper. Melt a little cooking oil and butter in a frying pan, add the zucchini, and fry gently for a few minutes until tender. Drain on kitchen paper. Serve hot.

CUCUMBER

Most widely used as a salad vegetable and eaten raw, although it can be cut in chunks and added to casseroles, or cooked in the same way as zucchini or celery. Cucumbers are usually bought *whole*. They keep best in the refrigerator wrapped in plastic wrap or a plastic bag.

Wash the cucumber. Peel thinly (if you wish) or leave unpeeled. Cut into thin slices and use with salad, or munch a chunk like an apple.

LETTUCE

Choose a lettuce that looks crisp and firm, with a solid heart; if it looks limp and flabby it is old and stale. Lettuce will keep for a few days in a plastic bag or a box in the refrigerator, but goes slimy if left too long; so buy *a small lettuce* unless you're going to eat a lot of salad.

Cut off the stalk and discard any brown or battered leaves. Pull the leaves off the stem and wash separately in cold, running water. Dry thoroughly in a salad spinner or clean dish towel. Put into a plastic bag or box in the refrigerator if not using immediately, to keep it crisp. Serve as a basic green salad (see page 108) or as a garnish with rolls, cheese, or cold meat, or as a side salad with hot dishes (alone or with a dressing).

SUMMER
SQUASH

A small squash will serve three or four people as a vegetable with meat or fish, or can be stuffed with meat or rice to make a dinner or supper dish.

Wash the squash in cold water. Cut into 1-inch rings or cubes, according to size. Boil or steam gently in salted water for 3 to 6 minutes until just tender. Drain very well, as squash can be a bit watery. (You can get the pieces really dry by shaking them in the pan over a very low heat for a few moments.) Serve with butter or tip the pieces into a greased oven-proof dish, top with grated cheese, and brown under a hot broiler. Squash can also be served with white, cheese, or parsley sauce (see page 221).

MUSHROOMS

Buy in small amounts so that they can be eaten fresh. Fresh mushrooms are pale-colored and look plump and firm; older ones look dried-up and brownish. Keep in the refrigerator. Mushrooms can be fried or broiled with bacon, sausages, chops, or steaks. Add them to casseroles or stews or make a tasty snack, cooking them in butter and garlic and serving on toast (see page 56).

Allow 2–3 mushrooms (1–2 oz.) per serving.

SAUTÉED
Brush or wipe with a cloth. Leave them whole, or slice large ones, if you wish. Fry them gently in a little butter and oil for a few minutes, until soft. They can be put in the frying pan with bacon or sausages, or cooked alone in a smaller saucepan.

BROILED
Put a small lump of butter in each mushroom and broil them for a few minutes in the base of the broiling pan. If you are broiling them with bacon, sausages, or chops, put them under the grill rack; the juice from the meat and mushrooms makes a tasty sauce.

OKRA

These curved seed pods can be served as a vegetable with meat or stew, or sautéed with tomatoes, onions, and spices with rice (see page 101) and served as a supper dish.

Allow 2 oz. per serving.

Slice the ends off the okra. Wash in cold water. Put 1–2 tbsp. cooking oil in a pan, add the okra and cook gently, stirring occasionally for 15 to 20 minutes until the okra feels tender when tested with a pointed knife. It should have a slightly glutinous texture.

ONIONS

The best way to peel onions without tears is to cut off the ends and then remove the skins with a vegetable knife under cold running water.

To chop onions evenly, slice them downward vertically into evenly-sized rings. If you want finely-chopped onion pieces, slice the rings through again horizontally. Sauté in butter, stirring frequently until soft and golden.

Combine with other cooked vegetables or a wide variety of dishes to give them added flavor.

Small onions (or large onions cut into quarters) can be cooked in the pan with a roast, alongside the potatoes.

PARSNIPS

These are very tasty and can be roasted on their own or with roast potatoes.

Allow 1 parsnip per person, if small, or cut a large parsnip into 5 or 6 pieces.

Parsnips are cooked in the same way as roast potatoes (see page 89), but do not cut them into too-small pieces or they get too crispy. If you peel them before you are ready to cook them, keep them covered in a pan of cold water, since they go brown very quickly. (If this should happen, the parsnips will still be all right to cook; they will just look a bit speckled.)

PEAS

Most commonly available canned or frozen nowadays. But fresh peas are a lovely treat in the summer, so try some.

Allow ½ lb. peas in the pod per serving.

Shell the peas and remove any that are discolored or spoiled. Boil them gently in salted water for 5 to 10 minutes. Drain well and serve with butter.

FROZEN PEAS

Allow 3–4 oz. per serving. Cook as directed on the package.

SNOW PEAS

Snow peas are also called sugar peas or podded peas.

Allow approximately ¼ lb. per serving.

Slice the ends off the peas with a vegetable knife and remove any strings. Wash and leave whole. Steam, or place in a pan of boiling, salted water and cook for 2 to 3 minutes. Peas are slightly crumbly when cooked. Serve hot with butter.

GREEN, RED,
OR YELLOW
PEPPERS

Use raw in a green salad, or cook, filled with rice or meat stuffing, for a lunch or supper dish (see page 111), or stewed in oil with tomatoes and garlic as a filling vegetable dish. Choose crisp, firm-looking peppers and store in the refrigerator.

Rinse in cold water, cut off the top and scoop out the core and seeds. Cut into rings or chunks and use in salad or as a garnish.

BOILED
POTATOES

Try to select potatoes of the same size to cook together, or cut large potatoes into evenly-sized pieces, so that all the potatoes will be cooked at the same time. (Very big potatoes will go soggy on the outside before the inside is cooked if left whole.) Do not let the water boil too fast or the potatoes will tend to break up.

Allow 2–4 potato pieces per person.

Peel the potatoes as thinly as you can. Dig out any eyes or any blemishes with as little waste as possible. Place in a pot, cover with hot water, and add a pinch of salt. Bring to a boil, lower the heat, and simmer for 15 to 20 minutes until they feel just soft when tested with a knife. Drain and serve hot.

MASHED POTATOES

The best way of serving boiled potatoes that have broken up during cooking. Prepare the boiled potatoes as described above. (If you are in a hurry, cut the potatoes into thick slices and cook for less time, approximately 10 minutes.) When they are cooked, drain well. Add warm milk and melted butter and mash with a fork or a masher until fluffy, then heap onto a serving dish.

POTATO CASTLES

Prepare mashed potatoes as above. Grease a flat baking pan or an oven-proof plate and pile the potatoes onto it in 2 or 3 evenly-sized heaps. Fork them into castles, top with a bit of butter, and either brown under the broiler for a minute or two or put them in a hot oven at 400° for 5 to 10 minutes until crisp and golden brown.

MASHED POTATOES WITH CHEESE

Prepare mashed potatoes as above, beating 1–2 oz. grated cheese into the potatoes with the butter. Pile the potatoes into a greased oven-proof dish, fork down evenly and top with a little grated cheese. Brown under a hot grill for a minute or two or put into a hot oven at 400° for 5 to 10 minutes until golden.

ROAST
POTATOES

These can be cooked around a roast or in a baking pan with a little hot grease to cook on their own.

Allow 2–4 potato pieces per person.

Peel the potatoes and cut them into evenly-sized pieces. Put them into a pot of hot water, bring to a boil, and simmer for 2 to 3 minutes. Put a little grease in a roasting pan. (Use margarine, drippings, or oil. Do not use butter on its own, as it burns and goes brown.) Heat the pan in the oven at 400–425°. Drain the potatoes and shake them in the pan over the heat for a moment to dry them. Put the potatoes into the hot roasting pan, taking care that the hot grease does not spit and burn you. Roast for 45 to 60 minutes, according to size, until crispy and golden brown.

NEW
POTATOES

Wonderful and easy—no peeling!

Allow 3–6 new potatoes, according to size and appetite.

Scrub the potatoes well under running water. If you prefer, scrape them with a vegetable knife also. Place in a pan, cover with boiling water, and add salt. Bring to a boil and simmer for 15 to 20 minutes until tender. Drain well, tip onto a plate, and top with butter.

SAUTÉED
POTATOES

A way of using up left-over boiled or roast potatoes. Potatoes can also be boiled specially and then sautéed when they are cold.

Allow approximately 3–4 cold cooked potato pieces, according to appetite.

Slice the potatoes thinly. Heat a little oil and butter in a frying pan. Add the potato slices and fry them gently for 5 minutes until crisp and golden, turning frequently.

ONION SAUTÉED POTATOES

Peel and thinly slice a small onion. Sautée in a frying pan with a little oil and butter until it is just soft, then add the cold, sliced potatoes and fry as above until crisp and delicious. Serve at once.

BAKED
POTATOES

These can be served as an accompaniment to meat or fish or made into a meal on their own, with any of numerous fillings heaped on top of them.

Allow 1 medium to large potato per person.

Choose potatoes that do not have moldy-looking patches on the skin. Remember that very large potatoes will take longer to cook, so if you are very hungry it's better to cook 2 that are medium-sized. Scrub the potato and prick several times with a fork.

TRADITIONAL WAY

Put the potato into the oven at 400° for 1 to 1½ hours, according to size. The skin should be crisp and the inside soft and fluffy when ready. Puncturing the potato halfway through cooking time will prevent it from bursting.

QUICKER WAY

Put the potato into a saucepan, cover with hot water, bring to a boil and cook for 5 to 10 minutes according to size. Drain it carefully, life the potato out with a cloth, and put into a 400° oven for 30 to 60 minutes, according to size, until it feels soft.

If you are cooking a casserole in the oven at a lower temperature, put the potato in the oven with it and allow extra cooking time.

BAKED
STUFFED
POTATO

Useful to serve with cold meat or with steak, as it can be prepared in advance and heated up at the last minute.

Scrub and bake a largish potato as described above. When the potato is soft, remove it from the oven and cut it carefully in half lengthways. Gently scoop the soft potato into a bowl and mash with a fork, adding a tbsp. butter and ½ oz. grated cheese. Pile the filling back into the skin again and fork down evenly. Place on a baking pan or oven-proof plate, sprinkle a little grated cheese on top, and either brown under the hot grill for a few minutes or put into a 400°) oven for 5 to 10 minutes until browned.

A FEW FILLING

Prepare and cook baked potatoes. When soft, put them onto a plate, split open, and top with your chosen filling.

Cheese
Cheese and onion
Cheese and relish
Cottage cheese
Baked beans
Spaghetti sauce
Bacon
Sour cream
Tuna fish
Curry sauce

SCALLOPED
POTATOES

Tasty and impressive-looking. Quick to prepare, but they take an hour to cook, so put them in the oven while you are preparing the meat or cook them on a shelf above a casserole in the oven. (The potatoes need a higher temperature, so put them on the top shelf and the casserole lower down.)

Allow 1–2 potatoes per person according to size and appetite.

Grease well an oven-proof dish. Peel the potatoes and slice them as thinly as possible. Put them in layers in the greased dish, sprinkling each layer with a little flour, salt and pepper. Almost cover them with ½–1 cup of milk (or milk and water). Dot generously with butter. Put the dish, uncovered, in a 400° oven for about an hour, until the potatoes are soft and most of the liquid has been absorbed. The top should be crispy.

Frozen scalloped potatoes are available in supermarkets. They are more expensive than making your own but are easy to prepare following the instructions on the package.

SPINACH

Allow 8 oz. per person. Spinach must be washed thoroughly in cold water to get rid of all dust and grit. This will take several rinses. Remove any tough-looking leaves and stalks and cut into convenient-sized lengths. Put the wet spinach in a large pot with no extra water and cook over a medium heat for 7 to 10 minutes until soft. As the spinach boils down, stir vigorously so that it cooks evenly in its own juices. Drain very well, pressing the water out to get the spinach as dry as possible. Reheat in the pan with butter and season well with salt and pepper.

FROZEN SPINACH
Allow 4 oz. per person. Packages of frozen spinach are available all year round in supermarkets. Cook as instructed and serve with butter.

RUTABAGAS
(SWEDES)

Known as "poisonous" by one member of our family, but really they are a delicious winter vegetable. Buy a very small rutabaga for one person, or a slightly larger one for 2 servings.

Peel thickly, so that no brown or green skin remains. Cut into ½ inch chunks. Cook uncovered in boiling, salted water for 15 to 20 minutes until tender. Drain well (if you are making gravy at the same time, save the water for the gravy liquid), and mash with a fork or potato masher, adding butter and plenty of pepper.

If you wish, peel one or two carrots, cut them into rings and cook them with the rutabaga, mashing the two vegetables together with butter as above, or just mixing the two together without mashing.

CORN

Frozen corn is available all year round. Cook as directed on the package. Fresh corn is in the stores in the summertime.

To cook corn on the cob, cut off the stalks and remove the leaves and silk threads. Put the ears into a large pot of boiling, unsalted water and simmer for 8 to 10 minutes until the kernels are tender. Drain and serve with plenty of butter by melting a little in the hot saucepan and pouring it over the ears.

Canned and frozen cut corn are also readily available.

SWEET POTATOES AND YAMS

Peel, boil and purée them like mashed potatoes (see page 92) or bake in a hot oven as you would an ordinary potato.

TOMATOES

"Love apples" add color and flavor to many dishes. They are used raw in salads or as a garnish, can be broiled, fried, chopped up and added to casseroles or stews, or stuffed as a supper dish. Choose firm tomatoes unless you are going to use them immediately.

Wash and dry the tomatoes, store in the refrigerator, and cut them into slices or quarters to use in a salad or as a garnish. Tomatoes are easy to cut or slice thinly if you use a bread knife or a vegetable knife with a serrated edge.

BROILED
Cut them in half, dot with butter, and broil for 3 to 5 minutes. Or put them under the broiler when grilling sausages, bacon, chops, or steak. The tomatoes will then cook with the meat.

SAUTÉED
Cut the tomatoes in half and sauté them on both sides in a little oil or grease, over a medium heat, for a few minutes until soft. Serve with bacon and sausages or on a slice of toast.

BAKED
Cut a cross in the top of any small or medium-sized tomatoes and halve any large ones. Put them into a greased, oven-proof dish with a lump of butter on top. Bake for 10 to 15 minutes at 350° until soft.

TURNIPS

Small white root vegetables.

Allow ½–2 turnips per serving, according to size and appetite.

Peel thickly. Leave small ones whole but cut large turnips in half or quarters. Cook them in boiling, salted water for 10 minutes or until soft. Drain well. Return the turnips to the pan and shake over a low heat for a few moments to dry them out. Serve with butter.

Turnips can also be served with diced carrots. Just peel them and cut them into large cubes, mix them with the carrots, and boil them together for 5 to 10 minutes. Drain and dry as above.

MASHED TURNIPS

Peel the turnips and cut them into chunks. Cook them in boiling water for 5 to 10 minutes until soft. Drain well and dry. Mash with a fork or potato masher with butter and pepper.

BOILED RICE

Use long grain rice, which keeps indefinitely in a jar or plastic container, or "easy cook" rice, which must be cooked exactly as described on the package. This kind is very good and easy to cook but is usually more expensive that plan long grain rice.

METHOD ONE

I prefer to use this method, since I tend to let the pan boil dry with the other one! However, you do need a largish pan, and it's a bit steamy. The rice must be cooked without the lin on or it boils over.

Preparation and cooking time: 13 minutes.

> **⅓ cup long grain rice**
> **½ tsp. salt**

Wash the rice well to get rid of the starch (put it into a saucepan and slosh it around in several rinses of cold water). Put the rice into a largish pan. Fill the pan two-thirds full of boiling water. Add the salt. Bring back to the boil and boil gently for 10 to 12 minutes, until the rice is cooked but still firm. Do not overcook. Drain well. Fluff with a fork and serve.

METHOD TWO

Be careful that the rice doesn't boil dry.

Preparation and cooking time: 13–16 minutes.

⅓ cup long grain rice
1 tsp. oil or butter
⅔ cup boiling water
Pinch of salt

Wash the rice as in method one. Put the oil or butter in a smallish saucepan and heat gently. Then add the rice, stirring all the time, to coat each grain. Add the boiling water and a pinch of salt, bring up to simmering point, and stir. Put on the lid and leave the rice to simmer over a very gentle heat for 15 minutes. Test to see if the rice is cooked: all the liquid should be absorbed and the rice should be cooked but not soggy. Lightly fluff with a fork and serve.

FRIED RICE

You can either use up leftover boiled rice (I always cook too much) or cook some specially.

Preparation and cooking time: 15 minutes (plus 15 minutes if you have to boil the rice first).

⅔ cup cooked boiled rice
½ onion or 2–3 scallions
½ slice cooked, chopped ham (optional)
1 tbsp. cooking oil
1 tbsp. frozen peas and/or corn (optional)

Peel and chop the onion, or wash and chop the scallions. (Scallions: cut off the roots and the dark green leaves and peel away the outer layer of the scallion. Chop.) Chop the ham. Heat the oil in a frying pan over a medium heat. Add the chopped onion and fry, turning frequently, until soft. Add the cooked rice and fry for 4 to 5 minutes, stirring all the time. Add the frozen peas (still frozen; they will defrost in the pan), corn, and ham, and cook for another 2 to 3 minutes, stirring all the time, until it is all heated through.

You can make this more substantial by adding more vegetables.

RISOTTO

A very cheap meal if you have any "pickings" of chicken left over. Otherwise buy a thick slice of cooked ham, chicken, or turkey to chop up. Risotto can be served with a green salad. (You do not need to include all the vegetables listed in this recipe; just choose whichever ones you prefer.)

Preparation and cooking time: 35 minutes.

> **1 hard-boiled egg**
> **1 cup rice**
> **1 small onion**
> **1 tbsp. oil or butter**
> **1 bullion cube**
> **1¼ cups boiling water**
> **1 slice cooked ham, chicken, or turkey**
> **2–3 mushrooms (sliced)**
> **1 tomato**
> **1 tbsp. frozen or canned peas**
> **1 tbsp. frozen or canned corn**
> **Salt and pepper**
> **Worcestershire sauce**
> **½ cup grated cheese**
> **Parmesan cheese (optional)**

Hard boil the egg for 10 minutes (see page 18). Wash the rice in several rinses of cold water. Peel and chop the onion finely. Heat the oil or fat in a medium saucepan or frying pan with a lid. Fry the onion for 3 to 4 minutes, until soft. Add the rice and fry, stirring well, for a further 3 minutes. Dissolve the bullion cube in the boiling water. Add this to the rice, stir, and leave to simmer with the lid on, stirring occasionally, for 10 to 15 minutes, until the rice is tender, and the liquid almost absorbed.

Chop the meat. Peel and chop the hard-boiled egg. Wash the sliced mushrooms. Wash and chop the tomato. Add the peas, corn, mushrooms, and tomato to the rice. Cook for 2 to 3 minutes, stirring gently. Then add the chopped meat and egg and continue stirring gently until heated right through. Season with salt, pepper, and Worcestershire sauce. Serve with lots of grated cheese and/or Parmesan and a dash of Worcestershire sauce.

RED
CABBAGE

Usually cooked in a casserole, to make a lovely warming winter vegetable dish. Why not put some baking potatoes in the oven to eat with it? (See page 92.)

Preparation and cooking time: 1 hour (cooked on top of the stove); 1 hour 15 minutes (cooked in the oven).

> **1 strip of bacon (optional)**
> **1 small onion**
> **½ small red cabbage**
> **1 eating apple**
> **1 tsp. oil**
> **1 tbsp. butter**
> **Salt and pepper**
> **1 tsp. sugar (brown if possible, but white will do)**
> **1 tsp. vinegar**
> **⅓ cup boiling water**

Chop the bacon with a sharp knife or a pair of scissors. Peel and chop the onion. Cut off the stalk from the cabbage. Remove any battered outside leaves. Shred the cabbage finely, wash, and drain. Peel, core, and slice the apple. Melt the oil and butter in a frying pan and fry the bacon until crisp. Remove the bacon, put it on a plate. Add the onion to the pan and fry gently for 2 to 3 minutes, until soft.

PAN METHOD
In a saucepan, put layers of the cabbage, apple, onion, and

bacon, seasoning each layer with salt, pepper, sugar and vinegar. Pour the boiling water over it and lightly sprinkle with sugar. Put on the saucepan lid and simmer gently for 45 minutes, stirring occasionally.

OVEN METHOD
Use a casserole dish (with a lid) that can be put in the oven. Put the vegetables in layers as in the pan method, adding the boiling water and the sugar, and bake at 350°, stirring occasionally, for about an hour. Potatoes can be baked along with the casserole. Serve hot. Red cabbage cooked in this way is tasty with pork and lamb.

BASIC
GREEN
SALAD

Preparation time: 5 minutes

3–4 washed lettuce leaves
½ small onion or a couple of scallions
1 tbsp. vinaigrette (see page 64)

Leave the lettuce leaves whole, if small, or shred as finely as you like. Peel and slice the onion. Put the lettuce and onion into a salad bowl, add the vinaigrette, and lightly turn the lettuce over in the dressing until well mixed. Other salad vegetables can be added: tomatoes (washed and sliced or cut into quarters); cucumber (washed and cut into rings or chunks); pepper (washed, cored, cut into rings); watercress (washed, sprinkled on top of the other vegetables); celery (washed, cut into one inch lengths); radishes (with tops cut off and roots removed, washed); scallions (wash, cut off roots and leaves and chop).

CREAMY
AVOCADO
TOAST

Use a soft avocado for this.

Preparation time: 5 minutes.

> **1 ripe avocado**
> **Salt and pepper**
> **2 thick slices of bread**
> **Butter**

Cut the avocado in half lengthways and remove the pit. Scoop out the soft flesh with a teaspoon, put it into a small bowl, and mash to a soft cream. Season with the salt and pepper. Toast the bread on both sides, spread one side with butter, then spread the avocado thickly on the top. Eat while the toast is hot.

SAVORY
AVOCADO
SNACK

Preparation and cooking time: 15 minutes.

1–2 strips of bacon
Oil (for frying)
1 small avocado
⅓ cup grated cheese
Chunk of French bread
Butter
Sliced American Cheese

De-rind the bacon. Fry it in a little oil in a frying pan over a moderate heat until crisp. Peel the avocado and slice it, removing the stone. Cut the French bread in half lengthways, and spread with the butter. Arrange layers of the avocado and bacon on the bread. Top with cheese slices or grated cheese. Broil for a few minutes until the cheese is golden, bubbling, and melted. Eat at once.

STUFFED
PEPPERS

Serve with a side salad and brown crusty bread.

Preparation and cooking time: 45 minutes.

> **1 small onion**
> **1 tbsp. oil (for frying)**
> **¼ lb. ground beef**
> **1 small tomato**
> **1 tsp. tomato purée (or ketchup)**
> **½ bullion cube**
> **⅓ cup boiling water**
> **Salt and pepper**
> **Pinch of herbs**
> **1 tbsp. raw rice or 2 tbsp. cooked rice if you have**
>   **any left over (optional)**
> **1–2 green peppers**

Peel and chop the onion. Heat the oil in a saucepan and fry the onion gently for a few minutes until soft. Add the ground beef and continue to fry for 2 to 3 minutes, stirring frequently. Wash and chop the tomato. Add it to the meat in the pan with the tomato purée (or ketchup).

Dissolve the bullion cube in the boiling water. Add it to the meat with the salt, pepper, and herbs. Continue simmering over a moderate heat. Stir in the washed raw rice and leave to simmer for 15 to 20 minutes, stirring occasionally. The stock should be almost completely absorbed. Cut the tops off the peppers. Remove the seeds and wash.

Grease an oven-proof dish. Remove the meat mixture from the heat. Strain off any excess liquid (the mixture should be damp but not swimming in gravy). If you are using rice, mix it in. Fill the peppers with the meat mixture and put them into the dish. Bake at 350° for 30 minutes.

VEGETABLE
HOT POT

This can be made with or without cheese to provide a tasty dish for lunch or supper, or it can be served as a vegetable accompaniment to meat to make a substantial meal, if you're really hungry. You can either buy fresh or raw vegetables, or use leftover vegetables. This recipe is particularly suitable for vegetarians.

Preparation and cooking time: 50 minutes.

> **1 small onion**
> **⅓–⅔ cup grated cheese (optional)**
> **2–3 potatoes**
> **Oil and butter**
> **1–2 cups mixed vegetables—carrots, cauliflower, celery, turnip, etc. Keep raw and cooked vegetables separate at this stage.**
> **⅔ cup vegetable soup**
> **Salt and pepper**

Peel and slice the onion. Peel the potatoes and cut them into ¼-inch slices. Heat the oil and butter in a saucepan over a moderate heat and sauté the onion for 2 to 3 minutes until soft. Add the raw vegetables (except the potatoes) and continue to fry gently for a few minutes. Stir in the soup. Bring to a boil, lower the heat, and simmer gently for 5 to 10 minutes until the vegetables are tender, adding any cooked vegetables for the last 2 to 3 minutes to heat them through.

Meanwhile, partly cook the sliced potatoes in boiling,

salted water for 4 to 5 minutes. Drain. Arrange the mixed vegetables in a casserole or oven-proof dish. Stir in half the cheese and cover with the hot soup. Season with salt and pepper. Top with a thick layer of potato slices. Dot with butter. Spring with the rest of the cheese. Bake at 400° for 15 to 20 minutes, until the top is golden brown. Serve hot.

VEGETABLE
CURRY

You can use fresh raw vegetables, left-over cooked vegetables, frozen vegetables, or a mixture of them all. Serve with boiled rice (see page 101).

Preparation and cooking time: 50 minutes.

> 1 small onion
> 1¼ cup mixed vegetables: carrots, cauliflower, potatoes, celery, rutabaga, turnip, etc. Keep the raw and cooked vegetables separate at this stage if you are using both.
> Oil for frying
> 1–2 tsp. curry powder (or to taste)
> ½ tsp. paprika pepper
> 1 tsp. tomato purée (or ketchup)
> 1 tsp. apricot jam (or red currant jelly)
> ½ tsp. lemon juice
> ⅔ cup milk (or milk and water)
> 1 tbsp. raisins, plain or golden
> 1 egg (optional)

Peel and chop the onion. Wash and prepare the fresh vegetables and cut them into largish pieces. Heat the oil in a saucepan over a moderate heat and fry the onion for a few minutes, stirring occasionally, until soft. Add the curry powder and paprika and cook, stirring as before, for 2 to 3 minutes. Stir in the tomato purée, apricot jam (or red currant jelly), lemon juice, milk and/or water and the raisins. Bring to a boil, reduce the heat, and leave to simmer with the lid on for 10 minutes.

Cook the raw or frozen vegetables in boiling water for 5 to 10 minutes. Drain. Hard-boil the egg (see page 18) in boiling water for 10 minutes. Then peel it and slice it thickly. Gently stir the vegetables into the curry sauce and simmer for a further 5 to 10 minutes, until the vegetables are completely cooked and the curry is hot. While the curry is simmering, cook the boiled rice. Garnish the curry with the hard-boiled egg.

COLESLAW

Quick and tasty way of using up extra raw cabbage. Serve with cold meat, or with hot dishes.

Preparation time: 15 minutes.

> **¼ crisp white cabbage**
> **1 small carrot**
> **1 eating apple (red-skinned if possible)**
> **Lemon juice (if possible)**
> **1 small onion**
> **1–2 tbsp. mayonnaise**
> **Salt and pepper**
> **Nuts, raisins, or green pepper (optional)**

Trim off the outer leaves and stalk of the cabbage. Shred it finely, wash it well in cold water. Scrape the carrot. Chop it finely or grate it. Peel and core the apple. Chop it finely or grate it. Sprinkle with a little lemon juice. Peel the onion. Chop or grate it finely. Drain the cabbage well. Mix all the vegetables together in a bowl. Toss lightly in the mayonnaise until all the ingredients are well coated. Season to taste.

Many different fruit or vegetables can be used in this recipe. A few chopped salted nuts, a tablespoon of washed, dried raisins, or a little chopped green pepper are some ideas you might like to try.

CRISPY
CABBAGE
CASSEROLE

This is filling enough to serve as a cheap supper dish with hot rolls, butter, and cheese. It is delicious as a vegetable accompaniment with meat.

Preparation and cooking time: 35 minutes.

> 1 quarter of a cabbage
> 1 small onion
> 1–2 stalks of celery
> 1 tsp. oil and 1 tbsp. butter (for frying)
> 1 slice of bread

For the white sauce:
> 1 tbsp. flour
> 1 cup milk
> 1 tbsp. butter (or margarine)
> Salt and pepper

Grease an oven-proof dish or casserole. Trim the outer leaves and stalk from the cabbage. Shred, not too finely, wash well, and drain. Peel and chop the onion. Scrape and wash the celery and cut into one-inch lengths. Heat the oil and butter in a frying pan and sauté the onions gently for 2–3 minutes until soft. Add the celery and drained cabbage and fry gently for a further 5 minutes, stirring occasionally.

Make the white sauce (see page 221). Put the vegetable

mixture into the greased dish. Pour the white sauce over the top. Crumble or grate the bread into crumbs and sprinkle on top of the sauce. Dot with butter. Bake for 15 minutes at 400° until the top is crunchy and golden brown.

BACON, SAUSAGE AND HAM

Lots of quick but substantial snacks in this chapter. Bacon and sausages don't take long to cook and are useful when you come home hungry and want a meal in a hurry.

BACON

Serve 1 to 2 strips of bacon per person. How well cooked you like your bacon is a very personal thing! As a rough guide, cook between 1 and 5 minutes. Tomatoes or mushrooms can be cooked in the broiler pan under the strips of bacon; the fat from the bacon will give them a good flavor.

Cut off the bacon rinds, if you wish.

BROILED
Heat the broiler. Put the bacon on the rack in the broiler pan and cook, turning occasionally, until it is cooked to your taste.

FRIED
Heat a smear of oil or fat in a frying pan. Add the bacon and fry over a medium-hot heat, turning occasionally.

SAUSAGES

These come in all shapes, sizes and pieces; the thicker the sausage, the longer it takes to cook.

Cook as many sausages as you can eat. Always prick them with a fork before cooking to keep them from bursting open.

BROILED

Heat the broiler. Put the sausages on the rack in the broiler pan and cook, turning occasionally, until brown and delicious (about 10 to 20 minutes). The thicker sausages may brown on the outside before the middle is cooked, so lower the oven rack away from the heat for the last 5 to 10 minutes of cooking time.

FRIED

Heat a smear of oil or fat in a frying pan over a medium heat (too hot a pan will make the sausages burst their skins), add the sausages, and fry gently, turning occasionally, until they are brown and crispy (10 to 20 minutes). Cook thick sausages for the longer time, using a lower heat if the outsides start getting too brown.

A PROPER
BREAKFAST

Tastes just as good for lunch or supper.

Preparation and cooking time: 20 minutes.

Use any combination of ingredients according to taste and appetite:

> **1–4 sausages**
> **1–2 strips of bacon**
> **1 tomato**
> **3-4 mushrooms**
> **1–2 left-over cold boiled potatoes**
> **1 tbsp. oil (for frying)**
> **1–2 eggs**
> **Butter**
> **Several slices of bread (for toast)**

Get everything ready before you start cooking: prick the sausages, de-rind the bacon, wash and halve the tomato, wash the mushrooms, and slice the potatoes. Warm a plate, put the kettle on for tea or make the coffee, get the bread ready to toast, and you're all set to start. Whether you use the broiler or a frying pan, start the sausages first, gradually adding the rest of the ingredients to the pan.

FRYING
Heat the oil in a frying pan over a moderate heat and fry the sausages gently, turning occasionally, allowing 10 to 20 minutes for them to cook according to size (see page 123).

When the sausages are half cooked, add the bacon and fry for 1 to 5 minutes until cooked to your taste. Push the sausages and bacon to one side or remove and keep warm. Put the potato slices into the pan and fry until crispy. Fry the tomato and mushrooms at the same time, turning them occasionally until cooked (4 to 5 minutes).

Remove the food from the pan and keep hot. Break the eggs into a cup and slide into the hot fat in the pan over a low heat. Fry them gently until cooked (see page 20). Remove them from the pan. Make the toast and tea and eat at once.

BROILING

Heat the broiler. Put the tomato halves and mushrooms in the bottom of the broiler pan, arrange the sausages above on the rack and broil until half cooked (5 to 10 minutes), turning to cook on all sides (see page 123). Arrange the bacon on the rack with the sausages and continue cooking for another 3 to 5 minutes, turning to cook both sides. Remove everything from the pan and keep it warm. Pour the fat from the grill pan into a frying pan, add extra oil or butter if necessary, then fry the potato slices and eggs as described above.

SAUSAGE
AND
MASHED
POTATO

Fast, filling, cheap and tasty!

Preparation and cooking time: 30 minutes.

> **2–3 potatoes—according to size and appetite**
> **2–4 sausages—according to size and appetite**
> **1 tbsp. butter**

Gravy:

> **1 tsp. flour and 1 tsp. instant gravy mix**
> **1 cup water (use the water the potatoes were**
>   **cooked in)**
> **A little grease from the sausages**

Peel the potatoes, cut into small, evenly-sized pieces, and cook in boiling, salted water for 10 to 20 minutes, according to size, until soft. Prick the sausages, cook under a hot broiler for 10 to 15 minutes, turning frequently, or fry over a medium heat with a smear of oil to keep them from sticking, turning often for 10 to 15 minutes until brown (see page 123). Test the potatoes for softness and drain them as soon as they are cooked. Mash them with a fork or potato masher and beat in the butter. Keep them warm

Make the gravy by mixing the flour and instant gravy

mix into a smooth paste with a little cold water, wine, sherry, or beer, etc. Add one cup of the vegetable water and any juices from the sausages. Pour the mixture into a small saucepan and bring to a boil, stirring all the time. Cook until the mixture thickens. Add more liquid if necessary (see page 220). Arrange the mashed potato on a hot plate, place the sausages around it, and pour the gravy over the top.

BRAISED
SAUSAGES

These take longer to cook but make a change from the usual fried or grilled sausages. Serve with mashed potatoes.

Preparation and cooking time: 50–60 minutes.

> **2–3 thick sausages (spicy Italian style)**
> **1–2 strips of streaky bacon**
> **1 small onion (or 2-3 scallions)**
> **2–3 mushrooms**
> **2 tsp. oil**
> **1 tsp. flour**
> **1 small cup wine or beer or ½ bullion cube**
> **dissolved in 1 cup boiling water**
> **Pinch of dried herbs**
> **Pinch of garlic powder**
> **Salt and pepper**

Prick the sausages. De-rind and chop the bacon. Peel and thickly slice the onion or scallions. Wash the mushrooms and slice if large. Heat the oil in a casserole or thick saucepan over a moderate heat and lightly brown the sausages. Remove them from the pan. Add the bacon and onion and fry for 2 to 3 minutes. Stir in the flour and gradually add the wine, beer, or stock, stirring as the sauce thickens.

Return the sausages to the pan. Add the mushrooms, herbs, garlic powder, salt, and pepper. Reheat, then put on the lid, lower the heat and leave to simmer gently for 35 to 45 minutes, removing the lid for the last 15 minutes of cooking time. Add a little more liquid if it gets too dry.

SAVORY
SAUSAGE
MEAT PIE

The apple gives the sausage meat a tangy taste.

Preparation and cooking time: 50 minutes.

> **3–4 potato pieces**
> **1 cooking apple**
> **1 onion**
> **2 tomatoes (canned or fresh)**
> **1 tsp. sugar**
> **4 oz. sausage meat (2–4 sausages)**
> **Butter**

Prepare the mashed potato (see page 87). Peel, core, and slice the apple. Peel and chop the onion. Slice the fresh tomatoes, or drain and slice the canned tomatoes. Place the apple slices in the base of a greased, oven-proof dish. Sprinkle with the sugar. If using sausages, slit the sausage skins to remove the sausage-meat, disposing the skins. Mix the chopped onion with the sausage-meat or the skinned sausages and spread over the apples.

Spoon the mashed potato around the dish to make a border or "nest" for the sausage. Cover the sausage with the tomatoes. Dot the potato with the butter and bake at 400° for 30 minutes, until the sausage is cooked and potato is crisp and golden-brown on top.

TOAD IN THE
HOLE

You can use either large sausages (toads) or little ones (frogs) for this meal, whichever you prefer! Some people believe that a better Yorkshire pudding is made if the ingredients are mixed together first and the batter is then left to stand in the refrigerator while you prepare the rest of the meal. Alternatively, make the batter while the sausages are cooking.

Preparation and cooking time: 45–55 minutes.

> **3–6 sausages (according to appetite and the size of the sausages)**
> **1 tbsp. cooking oil**

Yorkshire pudding batter:
> **2 heaped tbsp. flour**
> **Pinch of salt**
> **1 egg**
> **⅔ cup milk**

Heat the oven to 425°. Prick the sausages. Put them into a baking pan with the oil. Do not use one with a loose base. Cook the little sausages for 5 minutes or the larger ones for 10 minutes.

Make the batter, if you have not already done so: put the flour and salt in a bowl, add the egg, and beat it into the flour, gradually adding the milk, to make a smooth batter. (This is easier with a hand or electric mixer, but with a bit of old-fashioned effort you can get just as good a result using a whisk, wooden spoon, or even a fork.) Pour the batter into the baking pan on top of the hot sausages. Bake for a further 20 to 25 minutes, until the Yorkshire pudding is golden. Try not to open the oven door for the first 10 to 15 minutes, so that the pudding will rise well. Serve at once.

SAUSAGE AND BACON HUBBLE BUBBLE

A tasty way of using up odds and ends from the refrigerator

Preparation and cooking time: 30 minutes.

> **2–3 cooked boiled potatoes**
> **1 small onion**
> **1 strip of bacon**
> **2–4 sausages**
> **2 tsp. oil (for frying)**
> **1 egg**
> **⅓ cup milk**
> **Salt and pepper**

Heat the oven to 375°. Grease an oven-proof dish. Slice the cooked potatoes. Peel and chop the onion. De-rind the bacon. Prick the sausages. Heat the oil in a frying pan and fry the sausages, bacon, and onion gently for 5 minutes, turning frequently. Place the potato slices in the dish. Arrange the onions, sausages, and bacon on top. Beat the egg with the milk, salt, and pepper in a small basin, using a whisk or fork. Pour the egg mixture over the top and bake in a hot oven for about 15 minutes, until the egg mixture is set.

BACON-STUFFED
ZUCCHINI
OR SQUASH

Preparation and cooking time: 1 hour

1 onion
¼ lb. bacon
1 tomato
2 tsp. cooking oil
½ tsp. dried mixed herbs
Salt and pepper
2 medium zucchini

Peel and chop the onion. Cut the rind from the bacon and cut or chop it into small pieces. Chop the tomato. Heat the oil in a frying pan, add the onion, and fry gently for 3 to 4 minutes until soft. Add the bacon and cook for a further 8 to 10 minutes, stirring well. Add the tomato, herbs, salt, and pepper.

Wash the zucchini in cold water and cut out a wedge along the length of each zucchini to leave a hollow. Set the wedges aside. Spoon the filling into the hollow. Put the zucchini carefully into a greased, oven-proof dish and top with the wedges. Cover with a piece of foil and bake at 350° for about 45 minutes. Serve with hot brown rolls and butter and a green salad.

SUMMER SQUASH
These are often fairly large, so increase the quantity of stuffing and make enough for several people. Remove a thick slice

from the top of the squash and set aside. Scoop out the seeds and fill with the prepared stuffing. Top with the "lid" you sliced off. Brush lightly with a little cooking oil or softened butter and carefully place on a greased baking dish. Bake at 350° for about 1 hour.

FARMHOUSE
SUPPER

A tasty way of using up cooked potato and food from the refrigerator to make a meal.

Preparation and cooking time: 20 minutes.

> **3–4 cooked, boiled potatoes (see page 87 if you don't have any cooked)**
> **1 small onion**
> **1–2 strips of bacon**
> **½ small green pepper**
> **⅓ cup grated cheese**
> **A little oil for frying**
> **1 tbsp. butter**
> **1–2 eggs**

Slice and dice the potatoes. Peel and chop the onion. De-rind and dice the bacon. Core and chop the pepper. Heat the oil in a frying pan, add the bacon, and fry gently for 3 to 4 minutes. Remove the bacon from the pan and set aside. Put the potatoes, onion, and green pepper into the hot fat in the pan, and continue to fry gently for 5 to 10 minutes, until lightly browned.

Mix the bacon with the vegetables and place in an oven-proof dish. Melt the butter in the pan and fry the eggs (see page 20). Carefully place the eggs on top of the vegetables and bacon. Cover with the grated cheese, and brown for a few minutes under a hot grill, until the cheese is bubbly. Serve at once.

COOKED MEATS

FRIED LIVER
AND BACON
WITH FRIED
ONIONS

Preparation and cooking time: 15 minutes.

4–6 oz. chicken liver
1 strip of bacon
1 onion
**A little oil (for frying) and 1 tbsp. butter (for
 frying)**

De-rind the bacon. Peel and slice the onion into rings.
Dry the liver on paper towels. Heat the oil and butter in a
frying pan over a moderate heat. Add the onion slices and fry
for 3 to 4 minutes, stirring frequently, until soft. Push the
onion to one side of the pan and stir occasionally while frying
the bacon and liver.

Put the bacon and liver in the hot fat in the pan and fry gently
for 3 to 5 minutes, turning frequently, until cooked to taste—liver
should be soft on the outside, not crispy. Remove the liver, bacon,
and onion from the pan and serve on a hot plate.

Either pour the meat juices from the pan over the liver
and serve with crusty new bread, or make gravy with the
juices and serve with boiled potatoes and a green vegetable.

SAVORY
CORNED
BEEF HASH

Every cowboy's favorite standby!

Preparation and cooking time: 30 minutes.

3–4 potatoes
½ small onion
2–4 oz. corned beef
Salt and pepper
1 tbsp. oil (for frying)
1 egg
1 tsp. tomato purée (or ketchup)
1 tbsp. hot water
A dash of Worcestershire sauce
A dash of Tabasco sauce

Peel the potatoes, cut into large cubes, and cook for 5 to 6 minutes in boiling, salted water until half cooked. Drain well. Peel and finely chop the onion. Dice the corned beef. Mix together the potato cubes, onion, and corned beef. Season with salt and pepper. Grease a frying pan well with oil and put the meat and potato mixture into the pan.

Beat the egg. Dissolve the tomato purée or ketchup in a tablespoon of hot water, beat this into the egg, add the Worcestershire and Tabasco sauces, then pour onto the meat mixture. Fry gently for about 15 minutes, stirring occasionally. Serve hot.

LIVER
SAVORY

Serve with creamy, mashed potatoes, plain boiled rice, or crusty rolls and butter, and a green salad.

Preparation and cooking time: 25 minutes.

> **4–6 oz. chicken liver**
> **⅓ cup cold milk**
> **1 onion**
> **Clove of garlic (or pinch of garlic powder or garlic paste)**
> **1 tbsp. butter (for frying)**
> **A little oil (for frying)**
> **1 tsp. flour**
> **1 tbsp. tomato purée (or tomato ketchup)**
> **Pinch of mixed dried herbs**
> **Salt and pepper**
> **½ bullion cube**
> **⅓ cup hot water**

Cut the liver into 1-inch strips. Peel and slice the onion. Peel and chop the fresh garlic.

Heat the butter and oil in a frying pan over a moderate heat and fry the onion for 2 to 3 minutes, stirring occasionally, until just soft. Add the liver pieces and fry gently, turning frequently to brown on all sides (3 to 5 minutes). Stir in the flour, garlic, tomato purée, herbs, salt, and pepper. Remove from the heat. Dissolve the bullion cube in the hot water. Gradually mix in the stock and milk, return to the heat, and stir continuously until the sauce thickens. Lower the heat, cover the pan, and leave to simmer for 10 minutes until the liver is tender.

LIVER
HOT POT

Serve hot with a green vegetable.
Preparation and cooking time: 1 hour.

> **4–6 oz. chicken liver (sliced)**
> **3–4 potatoes**
> **1 onion**
> **1 tomato**
> **2–3 mushrooms**
> **Oil (for frying)**
> **Salt and pepper**
> **Pinch of dried herbs**
> **½ stock cube**
> **⅓ cup hot water**
> **Butter**

Peel the potatoes, slice them thickly and cook for 5 minutes in boiling, salted water until partly cooked. Drain them. Peel and slice the onion into rings. Wash and slice the tomato and mushrooms. Heat the oil in a frying pan and fry the onion rings gently for 2 to 3 minutes until just soft. Push them to one side of the pan. Add the liver slices and fry these, turning to cook both sides, for 1 to 2 minutes.

Grease an oven-proof dish or casserole and arrange the slices of onion, liver, mushrooms, and tomato in layers. Sprinkle with the salt, pepper, and herbs. Dissolve the stock cube in the hot water and pour the stock into the casserole. Cover the casserole with a thick layer of the sliced potatoes. Dot the potatoes with the butter, and bake at 375° for about 35 to 45 minutes, until the potatoes are brown and crispy on the top.

FISH

Fresh or frozen fish can be used in these recipes according to availability. Many commercially-frozen fish dishes sold in the supermarkets are quick and easy to cook. Follow the instructions given on the package carefully (short cuts aren't usually very successful) and serve with boiled or mashed potatoes, fresh or frozen vegetables, bread rolls or a side salad.

FRIED FISH
WITH BUTTER

Served with plain boiled potatoes.

Preparation and cooking time: 15–20 minutes (according to the type of fish used).

>   **2–4 potato pieces**
>   **6–8 oz. fillet of white fish (fresh or frozen)—cod,**
>   **haddock, etc.**
>   **2–4 tbsp. butter**
>   **1 tsp. cooking oil**
>   **Parsley (optional)**
>   **Slice of lemon (optional)**

Peel and boil the potatoes (see page 87). Wash and dry the fish. Melt the butter in a frying pan with the oil (the oil stops the butter from going too brown), add the fish and fry until tender (about 5 to 10 minutes), spooning the melted butter over the fish as it cooks. (The thicker the fish the longer it will take to cook.) Lift the fish carefully onto a warm plate, add a little chopped parsley (if used) to the butter in the pan and heat thoroughly. Pour the buttery juice over the fish and garnish with the lemon slice. Drain the potatoes and serve.

FRIED OR GRILLED TROUT (OR MACKEREL)

These can be bought fresh or frozen and provide a filling meal with just bread and butter.

Preparation and cooking time: 15–20 minutes

> **1 trout or mackerel**
> **1 tsp. oil (for frying)**
> **1 tbsp. butter**
> **Slice of lemon (optional)**
> **Vinegar (optional)**

The fish should be cleaned, with head, entrails, fins and gills removed. Supermarket fresh and frozen fish is already cleaned.

SAUTÉED
Heat the oil and butter in a frying pan and fry the fish over a moderate heat for about 5 minutes on each side.

BROILED
Dot with the butter and broil on both sizes until done (about 5 minutes each side for a medium-sized fish).

Serve with a slice of lemon and brown or French bread and butter.

COD STEAKS
WITH CHEESE

Use thick pieces of cod or haddock, or frozen fish steaks.

Preparation and cooking time: 20 minutes.

> **6–8 oz. piece cod (or 1–2 frozen fish steaks)**
> **Salt and pepper**
> **½ slice bread**
> **¼ cup grated cheddar cheese**
> **1 tbsp. butter**

Wipe the fish and season with salt and pepper. Grate or crumble the bread, grate or finely chop the cheese, and mix together. Put the fish in the base of a greased grill pan, dot with half the butter, and grill for 5 minutes. Turn the fish over, cover with the cheese mixture, dot with the remaining butter, and grill for another 5 minutes. Serve on a warm plate.

TOMATO
FISH BAKE

Preparation and cooking time: 35 minutes.

1 portion (6 oz.) fillet cod or haddock
2 tsp. cooking oil
½ small onion
**4 oz. canned tomatoes (or use 1 or 2 fresh
    tomatoes)**
Salt and pepper
¼ green pepper (optional)
1 stick celery (optional)

Put the fish in a greased oven-proof dish. Heat the oil in a small saucepan, chop the onion and fry it gently in the oil, until soft (2 to 3 minutes). Add the canned tomatoes or chopped fresh tomatoes and seasoning. Bring to a boil and cook gently until the liquid is reduced to a thin purée (3 to 5 minutes). Chop the celery and/or pepper if used, stir into the tomato mixture, and spoon the sauce over the fish. Cover with a lid or aluminum foil and bake for about 20 minutes at 375°. Serve hot.

TUNA BAKE

Serve with crispy rolls or toast.

> **1 can tuna fish**
> **⅔ cup condensed mushroom soup**
> **1 slice of bread (crumbled into bread crumbs)**
> **2 tbsp. butter**
> **A few mushrooms (optional)**

Drain the tuna fish and flake it into large flakes. Heat the soup in a saucepan, add the fish, and cook for 2 to 3 minutes. Pour the mixture into a heat-proof dish. Sprinkle with the breadcrumbs and dot with half the butter. Grill for 5 minutes or until golden brown. Meanwhile wash the mushrooms if used, melt the remaining butter in a pan, add the mushrooms, and cook gently for 4 to 5 minutes. Place on top of the hot tuna bake and serve at once.

Do not leave the remainder of the soup in the can. Put it into a covered container or cup in the refrigerator and use within 24 hours.

TUNA FIESTA

Serve with boiled rice or mashed potatoes.

Preparation and cooking time: 25 minutes.

> ⅓ cup long grained rice, or 2–4 potato pieces
> 1 small onion
> 1 tbsp. margarine (or butter or 1 tsp. cooking oil)
> 2 oz. mushrooms
> ½ green pepper
> ½ cup peas
> 2 tbsp. canned tomato soup
> Salt and pepper
> Garlic powder
> ½ can (about ⅓ cup) tuna fish (use the rest for
>   sandwiches)

Peel the potatoes (or wash the rice) and boil (see pages 87 and 101). Peel and slice the onion and fry it gently in the butter or oil in a saucepan, until soft (2 to 3 minutes). Wash and slice the mushrooms and pepper. Add them to the onion and fry gently, until soft (2 minutes). Add the peas, tomato soup, salt, pepper, and garlic. Gently stir in the drained tuna and cook for a few minutes, until hot. Strain the potatoes and mash (or drain and fork the rice). Spoon the potatoes or rice onto a plate, press into a ring and pour the tuna sauce into the middle.

Do not leave the remainder of the tuna fish or soup in the cans. Put them into cups in the refrigerator and use within 24 hours.

COD IN
WHITE WINE

Preparation and cooking time: 30-35 minutes.

1 small onion
Slice of lemon (optional)
Salt and pepper
6–8 oz. piece of cod (or 1–2 frozen fish steaks)
½ cup white wine
½ slice of bread
1 tbsp. butter

Grease an oven-proof dish. Peel and slice the onion finely, and arrange half in the dish. Add a squeeze of lemon, salt and pepper. Put the fish on top and cover with the rest of the onion and another squeeze of lemon. Carefully pour in the wine. Crumble the bread into crumbs and sprinkle on top of the fish. Dot with the butter. Bake at 375° until golden brown.

BEEF

BEEF
CASSEROLE
OR STEW

You can use any mixture of stewing beef and vegetables to make a casserole (cooked in the oven) or a stew (simmered in a covered pan on top of the stove), so just combine the vegetables you like. If you want the meal to go further, add extra vegetables. Since this dish is easier to cook in larger quantities, why not double or triple the ingredients to make enough for 2 or 3 friends?

Preparation and cooking time: 1 hour, 50 minutes to 2 hours, 50 minutes. (For one person, cook 4 oz. stew beef for 1 hour, 30 minutes; for 2 people cook 8 oz. stew beef for about 2 hours; for larger quantities, cook for 2 hours, 30 minutes.)

> **1 onion**
> **A little oil or grease (for frying)**
> **4–6 oz. stew beef**
> **Bullion cube**
> **½ cup of wine or beer (optional)**

Vegetables—any mixture according to taste:
> **1 carrot—peeled and sliced**
> **Small turnip—peeled thickly, cut into 1-inch chunks**
> **Stalk of celery—washed and cut into ½-inch lengths**
> **½ green pepper—washed, with the core and seeds removed, cut into short strips**

1 zucchini (or 1 small eggplant)—washed, cut
    into ½-inch pieces
1 potato—peeled, cut into 1-inch chunks
1 oz. mushrooms—washed, sliced
Clove of garlic—peeled, finely chopped
Cup of water
Pinch of herbs
Garlic powder
Salt and pepper

Peel and slice the onion and fry it gently in a casserole or a saucepan until soft (about 2 to 3 minutes). Cut the meat into 1-inch pieces, add to the onion in the pan, and fry until brown (3 to 5 minutes) stirring so that it cooks evenly. Stir in the bullion cube and add the wine or beer if used.

Prepare the vegetables but do not cut them too small. Add them to the meat. Stir in the water so that it just covers the meat and vegetables. Add the herbs, salt, pepper, and garlic powder. Bring to a boil and stir well. Then either put the covered casserole dish in the middle of a moderate oven (375°), or lower the heat and leave to simmer with the lid on the pan for 1½ to 2½ hours according to the amount of meat used, stirring occasionally. If it seems to be drying up, add a little more wine, beer, or water.

Serve very hot, on its own or with baked potatoes (cooked in the oven with the casserole), boiled potatoes, or hot French bread and butter.

SHEPHERD'S
PIE

For a change, add a little grated cheese to the potato topping and sprinkle the top with grated cheese before grilling. The meat mixture can also be served on its own or with boiled or mashed potatoes and vegetables.

Preparation and cooking time: 55 minutes.

> **1 small onion**
> **2 tsp. oil (for frying)**
> **¼ lb. ground beef**
> **A little wine or beer (if you have any opened)**
> **2 tsp. ketchup (optional)**
> **Shake of Worcestershire sauce (optional)**
> **½ bullion cube**
> **⅓ cup water**
> **2–3 potatoes**
> **1 tbsp. butter or margarine**
> **1 tomato (optional)**

Peel and chop the onion. Put the oil in a saucepan and fry the onion gently for 2 to 3 minutes until soft. Add the meat and continue to fry gently, stirring all the time, until the meat is brown (about 2 to 3 minutes). Add the wine or beer and sauces, bullion cube, and water. Stir well. Bring to a boil, then reduce the heat and leave to simmer for 20 to 30 minutes, until the meat is tender.

Meanwhile, peel the potatoes, cut them into evenly-sized pieces, and cook in boiling, salted water for 15 to 20 minutes, until soft. Drain and mash them with a potato masher or fork. Add the butter and beat until creamy. Pour the meat mixture into an oven-proof dish, cover with the mashed potato, and fork down smoothly. Dot the top with a little butter, top with a sliced tomato, if liked, and broil for a minute or two until golden brown, or put on the top shelf of a hot oven (400°) for 5 to 10 minutes until it is brown on top.

POTATO
BOLOGNESE

For those of you who don't like pasta or who want a change from spaghetti.

Preparation and cooking time: 45 minutes.
Traditional Bolognese sauce (see page 203).

> **3–4 potatoes**
> **1 tbsp. of butter**
> **1 oz. grated cheese (or Parmesan cheese)**

Prepare the Bolognese sauce and leave to simmer. Peel and slice the potatoes thickly and cook in boiling, salted water for 10 minutes, until soft (see page 87). Drain and mash the potatoes with the butter, beating them well. Pile them onto a hot dish, forming them into a border or "nest." Pour the Bolognese sauce into the potato nest. Serve with grated or Parmesan cheese.

BEEF CURRY

This is a medium-hot curry and is easier to prepare for two or more people, as very small amounts tend to dry up during cooking. Why not try doubling the quantity?

Preparation and cooking time: 1 hour, 50 minutes to 2 hours, 50 minutes. (For one person cook ¼ lb. stew beef for 1 hour, 30 minutes; for 2 people cook ½ lb. stew beef for about 2 hours; for larger quantities cook for 2 hours, 30 minutes.)

1 onion
4–6 oz. stew beef
A little cooking oil (for frying)
2 level tsp. curry powder (more or less according to taste)
1 small apple (preferably a cooking apple)
1 tomato
½ bullion cube and 1 cup boiling water (or 5.2 oz. mulligatawny soup)
2 tsp. golden raisins
1 tsp. sugar
2 tsp. relish or chutney

Peel and slice the onion. Cut the beef into 1-inch cubes. Heat the oil in a medium-sized saucepan and fry the onion gently, to soften it, for 3 to 5 minutes. Add the beef and fry for another 5 minutes until browned. Sprinkle the curry powder over the meat and stir for a few minutes over a medium heat. Peel and chop the apple, wash and chop the tomato, add both to the meat, and continue frying for 3 to 4 minutes, stirring gently.

Dissolve the stock cube in 1 cup of boiling water and add the stock to the meat, or add the mulligatawny soup. Wash and drain the raisins. Add them to the curry with the sugar and relish or chutney. Stir well and simmer gently, with the lid on, stirring occasionally, for 1½ to 2½ hours until the meat is tender. Serve with plain boiled rice (see page 101), poppadums, and some side dishes (see below).

SIDE DISHES FOR CURRIES

  Salted nuts
  Chopped green peppers
  Plain yogurt
  Chopped tomatoes
  Sliced onions
  Sliced banana (sprinkle with lemon to keep it white)
  Chopped apple
  Chopped cucumber
  Chopped, hard-boiled egg
  Washed, drained golden raisins
  Mango chutney
  Shredded coconut

POPPADUMS

Great fun to cook. Buy a package of Indian poppadums, available at large supermarkets. Heat 3–4 tbsp. cooking oil in a frying pan over a medium heat (enough to cover the base of the pan). When the oil is hot, float a poppadum on top and it will puff up immediately, taking only a few moments to cook. Remove it carefully and leave it to drain on paper towels while cooking the next poppadum. Do not let the fat get too hot, or it will get smoky and burn.

HOME-MADE
HAMBURGERS

A change from fast food. You can make them bun-sized or "half pounders."

Preparation and cooking time: 20–25 minutes according to size.

> ½ small onion
> 4-8 oz. ground beef, according to appetite
> Salt and pepper
> Pinch of dried herbs
> Worcestershire (or Tabasco) sauce
> A little beaten egg (or egg yolk)
> A little oil (for frying)

Peel and finely chop the onion and mix well in a bowl with the ground beef, using a fork. Mix in the salt, pepper, herbs, and sauce and bind together with a little egg. The mixture should be wet enough so the ingredients mold together, but not soggy. Divide this into 2 portions, shape each into a ball, and then flatten into a circle, about ¾ inch thick.

Heat the oil in the frying pan over a medium heat. Put the hamburgers carefully in the pan and fry for 10 to 15 minutes, according to size, turning occasionally to cook both sides. Do not have the heat too high, as the hamburgers need to cook through to the middle without burning the outside. Serve in buns with ketchup or barbecue sauce, or with potatoes, vegetables or a salad.

BEEF
STROGANOFF

Absolutely delicious, and very impressive if you have a special friend to dinner. This recipe makes enough for *two* people. Serve with plain boiled rice, noodles, or new potatoes, and a salad.

Preparation and cooking time: 25 minutes.

> **1 cup plain boiled rice (or 2 cups noodles or 3–6 new potatoes)**
> **8 oz. fillet (or rump steak)**
> **1 medium onion**
> **1 tbsp. butter (or a little cooking oil)**
> **4 oz. mushrooms**
> **1 small green pepper**
> **Salt and pepper**
> **Garlic powder**
> **3–4 tbsp. sour cream (or heavy cream or plain yogurt)**
> **Chopped parsley**

Cook the rice, noodles or scrubbed new potatoes in boiling salted water (see page 101, 199, 87). Cut the beef into thin strips, 2 inches long by ½ inch by ¼ inch. Peel and finely chop the onion and sauté in half the oil or butter in a frying pan or wok until soft (2 to 3 minutes). Wash and slice the mushrooms. Wash the pepper, remove its core and seeds, and cut it into strips. Add the mushrooms and the pepper to the frying pan and fry gently for another 4 to 5 minutes.

Remove all the vegetables from the pan and place on a plate. Melt the remaining butter or oil in the pan, add the beef strips, and fry for 3 to 4 minutes, turning frequently so that they cook evenly. Return the onion, pepper and mushrooms to the pan. Add the salt, pepper and garlic powder. Gently stir in the sour cream, or yogurt and mix well. Heat carefully until piping hot, but try not to let the sauce boil. Sprinkle with chopped parsley. Drain the rice, noodles, or potatoes and serve at once.

CHILI CON
CARNE

This is another dish that is easier to make in larger quantities than are given below, so if possible, double the ingredients and cook for 2 people. You can use ground beef or stew beef.

Preparation and cooking time: 2 hours, 55 minutes (if using stewing steak); 1 hour, 25 minutes (if using ground beef).

> 1 small onion
> 1 clove of garlic (or a little garlic powder)
> A little cooking oil
> ½ tbsp. butter
> 1 strip of bacon (or bacon trimmings)
> ¼ lb. stew beef or ground beef
> 1 tbsp. tomato purée (or ketchup)
> 1 cup water
> Salt and pepper
> ½ level tsp. chili powder
> 1 cup canned cooked red kidney beans or 4 oz.
>   pre-cooked kidney beans (boiled for half an
>   hour in fast boiling water, then drained)
> A few drops Tabasco sauce (optional)

Peel and chop the onion and garlic. Put the oil and butter into a saucepan. Add the onion and fry gently until soft (2 to 3 minutes). Cut the bacon into small pieces. Add the bacon and beef to the pan and fry until browned, stirring so that it cooks evenly. Add the tomato purée (or ketchup), water, salt, pepper, and chili powder. Bring to a boil. Cover, lower the heat, and leave to simmer for 1 hour (if using ground beef) or 2½ hours (if using stew beef), stirring occasionally and adding a little extra water if it gets too dry. Add the kidney beans. Simmer for another 10 minutes. Taste (but be careful not to burn your tongue) and add Tabasco sauce if desired. Serve hot.

BROILED (OR PAN-FRIED) STEAK

Grilled tomatoes and mushrooms are tasty with steak (see below). Serve with baked potatoes, sautéed potatoes, boiled potatoes, backed stuffed potatoes, or rolls, and a salad or frozen peas. Prepare the vegetables before cooking the meat, as steak is best eaten as soon as it is ready. To cook the vegetables, see the chapter on vegetables (page 59). Broiling is the best way to cook steak, but it can be fried, too.

CUTS OF BEEF TO CHOOSE

Rump — Good flavor, quite lean. Cut it into thick portions ¾ inch at least

Sirloin — Very tender, with some fat. Cut as rump.

Fillet — Very tender, very expensive! Cut into even thicker portions 1-1½ inches so that it stays juicy during cooking.

For more steak options, ask the butcher at your supermarket.

Preparation time: 2–3 minutes. Cooking time: see method.

Allow 6–8 oz. steak per serving.
A little cooking oil (or butter)

BROILED
Heat the broiler. Put the steak on the greased rack of the

broiler pan and brush or wipe it with the oil or butter. Cook on one side, then turn it over carefully (do not stab the meat). Brush or wipe the second side with the oil or butter and cook to suit your taste:

Minute steak — 1 minute cooking each side.

"Rare" steak — 2–4 minutes each side, depending on thickness.

Medium steak — Cook as "rare," then lower the heat for another 3–4 minutes each side.

Well done steak — Cook as "rare," then lower the heat for another 4–5 minutes each side.

PAN-FRIED

Heat the frying pan gently. Put a little oil or fat in the pan. Add the steak, and cook over a medium-high heat, as for steak above. Serve immediately with chosen vegetables.

Cut tomatoes in half and grill under the steak in the grill pan, or fry in the frying pan with the meat, for 3 to 5 minutes. Mushrooms are best cooked in the bottom of the grill pan with a little butter, with the meat juices dripping onto them, or they can fry in the frying pan with the steak. They will take from 3 to 5 minutes, according to size.

KEBABS

Served with boiled rice (see page 101) or rolls and a green salad and barbecue sauce.

Preparation and cooking time: 20–25 minutes.
The following measurements are for one person. Use any mixture of the following:

> ¼ lb. beef or lamb (cubed)
> 2–4 button mushrooms
> 1–2 tomatoes
> A few pieces of green pepper
> 1 onion
> 1–2 long skewers
> Oil for cooking

Heat the oven to 400° or preheat the broiler. Cook the rice, if used, in boiling, salted water. Assemble and prepare your chosen ingredients as follows. Wash the mushrooms. Wash the tomatoes and cut into halves or quarters, according to size. Slice the green pepper into chunks. Peel the onion and cut into quarters.

Thread the skewers with the chosen food, arranging it as you wish. Brush with oil. Either broil, taking care not to place skewers too close to the heat, or balance the skewers across a baking pan in the hot oven and cook for about 15 minutes, turning frequently. Drain the rice. Prepare the salad. Serve the kebabs on the skewers—be careful: they will be hot, so have a napkin handy.

CHICKEN

Frozen chicken must be thoroughly defrosted before you start cooking. Defrost frozen chicken in the refrigerator. This takes 2–3 days for a whole chicken, but is much safer than defrosting at room temperature because it prevents the growth of salmonella and other dangerous bacteria. You can hasten the defrosting process by putting the nearly-thawed chicken in a bowl of cold (not hot) water to get ride of all the ice crystals. Change the water frequently to keep it cold. Chicken defrosted too quickly in hot water can also grow bacteria and will be tough when cooked. If chicken is not completely thawed before cooking it may not cook right through and any bacteria present will not be destroyed and could then make you ill.

Chicken must be cooked thoroughly, too. The juices should run clear, not tinged with pink, when pierced with a knife at the thickest part of the joint.

FRIED
CHICKEN

A quick and easy dinner, served with new or sautéed potatoes and peas or a green salad. It is also tasty when eaten with fresh rolls and butter.

Preparation and cooking time: 20–22 minutes, plus defrosting time.

> **1 chicken breast or leg quarter — 6–8 oz.
> according to your appetite
> A little oil and butter (for frying)**

Wash the chicken pieces and dry them on paper towels. Heat the oil and butter in a frying pan over a moderate heat, add the chicken, and fry it gently for 15 to 20 minutes, according to size, turning it occasionally so that it browns on both sides. If the chicken seems to be getting too brown, lower the heat but continue cooking to ensure that it cooks all the way through. Remove from the pan. Serve hot or cold.

CHICKEN IN
TOMATO
AND
MUSHROOM
SAUCE

Fried chicken served in a tasty sauce. This dish is good with boiled rice or potatoes, which can be cooked while the chicken is frying.

Preparation and cooking time: 40 minutes, plus defrosting time.

> 1 chicken breast or leg quarter—6-8 oz.
>   according to you appetite
> A little oil and butter (for frying)
> ½ small onion
> 2-3 mushrooms
> ½ bullion cube
> ½ cup hot water
> 2 tsp. tomato purée (or tomato ketchup)
> Pinch of dried mixed herbs
> Salt and pepper
> Pinch of garlic powder

Fry the chicken as in previous recipe. Remove to a warm dish and keep hot.

Peel and chop the onion, put it into the oil in the frying pan, and fry gently for 2 to 3 minutes until soft. Wash and

slice the mushrooms and add to the onion. Dissolve the bullion in the hot water, add to the onion in the pan, bring to a
boil, stirring all the time, then reduce the heat and cook for
another 5 minutes. Add the tomato purée, herbs, seasoning,
and garlic powder, and continue cooking for another 4 to 5
minutes—the sauce should now be thick and will coat the
chicken. Pour the sauce over the chicken. Serve with rice or
potatoes.

CHICKEN
WITH CORN—
FOR 2

The corn and potato sauce turns fried chicken into a complete meal.

Preparation and cooking time: 25–30 minutes, plus defrosting time.

> **2 chicken breasts or leg quarters**
> **A little oil and butter (for frying)**
> **1 onion**
> **10 oz. new potatoes, peeled**
> **11½ oz. cut corn, canned or frozen**
> **1 tbsp. butter**
> **2 tsp. flour**
> **⅔ cup milk**
> **Salt and pepper**

Fry the chicken as in preceding recipes. While the chicken is frying, make the sauce. Peel and slice the onion. Boil the potatoes until soft, and drain. Drain the corn, if canned. Melt the butter in a saucepan over a moderate heat and fry the onion gently for 2 to 3 minutes. Add the boiled potatoes and cook for another 5 minutes, stirring gently.

Add the corn and mix well. Stir in the flour, and cook for 2 to 3 minutes. Remove from the heat and gradually add the milk. Return to the heat and bring to a boil, stirring until the sauce thickens. Simmer for a few minutes, stirring gently, trying not to break up the potatoes. Season the sauce with the salt and pepper. Put the chicken onto a warm serving dish, cover with the sauce, and serve at once.

ROAST
CHICKEN
PIECES

A quick and economical roast dinner. The chicken pieces are cooked in a roasting pan in the oven in the same way as a whole roast chicken and can be served with stuffing (see page 226), apple sauce (see page 224), roast potatoes (see page 89), and vegetables.

Preparation and cooking time: 35–45 minutes according to size, plus defrosting time.

> **Quarter of a chicken (breast or leg) or 2 chicken pieces**
> **2 tsp. oil and 1 tbsp. butter (for cooking)**
> **Dried herbs (optional)**
> **Aluminum foil**

Heat the oven to 400°. Rub the chicken with the oil and dot with the butter. Sprinkle with herbs, if liked. Place in a well-greased roasting pan and cover with aluminum foil. Roast for 30 to 40 minutes, according to the size of the chicken pieces, until the juices run clear (not pink) when tested with a fork. (If still pink, cook for a few more minutes.) Remove the foil for the last 10 minutes of cooking time to brown the chicken. Sausages, roast potatoes, and parsnips can be cooked around the chicken pieces. Remove the chicken, and the sausages, potatoes, and parsnips (if used) from the pan and keep warm. Use the juices left in the pan to make the gravy (see page 220).

EASY CHICKEN CASSEROLE— FOR 2

Make this for 2 people or the sauce will dry up before the chicken is cooked. It can be prepared very quickly and popped into the oven. Put a couple of baking potatoes to cook in the oven with it, and you have a complete meal.

Preparation and cooking time: 1 hour, 10 minutes, plus defrosting time.

> **2 chicken breasts or leg quarters**
> **A little oil (for frying)**
> **4 oz. canned or frozen mixed vegetables**
> **⅓ cup condensed chicken soup**
> **Salt and pepper**
> **Garlic powder or paste (optional)**

Heat the oil in a frying pan over a moderate heat and fry the chicken for 5 minutes, turning so that it browns on all sides. Remove and place into a casserole with the frozen vegetables. Heat the soup in the pan with the chicken juices, adding the seasoning and garlic. Pour this sauce over the chicken. Cover with a lid and cook for about an hour until the chicken is tender, either in the over at 350° or over a very low heat on top of the stove.

CHICKEN
CURRY

Use the recipe for beef curry (page 157), substituting a chicken quarter for the stew beef. Chicken cooks more quickly than beef, so the curry only needs to simmer for an hour. Serve with boiled rice (see page 101) and curry side dishes as suggested on page 158.

HAWAIIAN
CHICKEN

Serve with new or sautéed potatoes or potato castles, and green beans or peas.

Preparation and cooking time: 40 minutes, plus defrosting time.

> ½ lb. chicken, with bone
> 1 tsp. oil and a tbsp. butter (for cooking)
> ½ cup canned pineapple pieces, chunks, or slices in syrup
> 1 tsp. flour
> 1 tsp. soy sauce
> 1 tsp. Worcestershire sauce

Heat the oil and butter in a frying pan and fry the chicken over a moderate heat for 10 minutes, turning occasionally so that it browns on all sides. Remove from the pan for a few minutes. Drain the pineapple, saving the syrup. Mix the flour into a smooth paste with a little of the syrup. Add the remainder of the syrup and stir into the juices in the frying pan, stirring until the sauce thickens. Return the chicken to the pan, add the pineapple pieces, and pour the soy sauce and Worcestershire sauce over the chicken. Stir well, then lower the heat and simmer for 15 minutes, stirring occasionally.

CHICKEN IN
WINE

This can be made with chicken on the bone but is terrific made with boneless chicken breast or filleted turkey, according to your taste. Serve with new potatoes and peas.

Preparation and cooking time: 45–60 minutes, plus defrosting time (chicken on the bone takes the longest time).

> **6–8 oz. chicken on the bone, boneless chicken breast, or slice of turkey fillet**
> **1 small onion**
> **1 bullion cube—preferably chicken flavor**
> **½ cup hot water**
> **1 tsp. oil and a tbsp. of butter**
> **⅓ cup white wine**
> **½ tsp. herbs**
> **Salt and pepper**
> **1 tsp. flour**

Peel and finely chop the onion. Dissolve the bullion cube in the hot water. Heat the oil and butter over a moderate heat, in a casserole or thick saucepan, and fry the chicken gently for a few minutes, turning it so that it browns on all sides. Remove from the pan. Add the onion to the pan and stir over the moderate heat for a few minutes to soften.

Pour most of the wine onto the onions, stir well, and allow to bubble for a minute. Return the chicken to the sauce. Stir in the stock, herbs, salt, and pepper (according to taste). Cover the pan, and simmer very gently for 30–45 minutes, until the chicken is tender. Mix the flour with the rest of the wine to make a smooth paste and gradually stir this into the chicken sauce until it has thickened a little. Serve hot.

LAMB

This chapter covers lamb chops and lamb stew—not the fancier leg or shoulder of lamb, which are covered in the chapter "Sunday Lunch Dishes."

LAMB CHOPS— BROILED OR FRIED

Choose lean chops, but remember that a little fat gives the meat a good flavor. Tomatoes, mushrooms, new potatoes, and peas go well with lamb. Traditionally, mint sauce (see page 225), mint jelly, red currant jelly, or onion sauce (see page 222) are served with lamb.

Preparation and cooking time: 12–17 minutes.

> **1 large or 2 small lamb chops**
> **A little oil**

BROILED

Heat the broiler. Brush or rub both sides of the chops with oil. Place on the greased rack of the broiler pan and broil for 8 to 10 minutes, according to the size of the chops and your preference, turning the meat so that it browns evenly on both sides. Lamb is traditionally served pink and underdone in the middle and brown and crispy on the outside, but cook the chops the way you like them.

PAN-FRIED

Heat a little oil in a frying pan over a medium heat. Place the chops in the pan and fry, turning several times, for 8 to 10 minutes until the chops are brown and crispy and cooked according to taste.

OVEN CHOP

Serve with a baked potato, which can cook in the oven with the casserole. This dish is just as good made with a pork chop.

Preparation and cooking time: 50–55 minutes.

> **1 small onion**
> **3–4 mushrooms**
> **½ tbsp. oil (for frying)**
> **1 large lamb chop**
> **½ cup canned tomatoes**
> **Salt and pepper**
> **Pinch of herbs**

Peel and slice the onion. Wash and slice the mushrooms. Heat the oil in a frying pan over a medium heat. Fry the onion for 3 to 4 minutes to soften it. Add the chop to the pan and cook on both sides for a few minutes to brown. Add the mushrooms and cook for another minute. Put the chop into a casserole or oven-proof dish and pour the onion and mushrooms over it.

Heat the tomatoes in the frying pan with the meat juices. Add these to the casserole with the salt, pepper, and herbs. Cover with a lid or aluminum foil. Bake at 400° for 45 minutes, removing the lid for the last 15 minutes to reduce and thicken the sauce. If serving with a baked potato, scrub and prick the potato and cook it in boiling water for 10 minutes. Drain. Place in the oven to bake with the casserole for 30 to 45 minutes, according to size.

IRISH STEW

This makes a substantial meal on its own but can be served with extra potatoes or rolls and a green vegetable.

Preparation and cooking time: 2 hours, 20 minutes to 2 hours, 50 minutes.

> ¾-1 lb. boned lamb
> 2 onions
> 2 carrots
> 1–2 potatoes
> 1 tbsp. oil (for frying)
> 1 bullion cube
> 2–3 cups boiling water
> ½ tsp. mixed herbs
> Salt and pepper

Cut the lamb into pieces suitable for serving. Trim off any large pieces of fat. Peel and slice the onions and carrots. Peel the potatoes and cut them into chunks.

Heat the oil in a large saucepan. Sauté the onion and carrots over a medium heat for 3–4 minutes, stirring occasionally. Add the meat and cook for another 2–3 minutes until the pieces are brown on all sides. Add the potato. Dissolve the bullion cube in 1 cup of boiling water and pour it over the meat, adding enough extra water to cover the meat and vegetables. Add the herbs, salt, and pepper. Stir gently and bring to a boil, then reduce the heat to a simmer. Cook slowly for 1½ hours with the lid on.

LAMB STEW

Preparation and cooking time: 2 hours, 15 minutes.

> 1 lb. boned lamb
> 2 onions
> 1 carrot
> 1 very small turnip (optional)
> 3 or 4 potatoes
> 1 tbsp. oil (for frying)
> 1 stock cube
> 2 cups boiling water (approximately)
> 2 tsp. flour
> Salt and pepper
> Pinch of dried herbs
> Butter

Cut the lamb into pieces suitable for serving. Peel and slice the onions, carrot, and turnip (if used). Peel and slice the potatoes and cut into thick slices.

Heat the oil in a frying pan and brown the lamb pieces over a medium heat, turning them so that they cook on all sides. Arrange in a casserole or oven-proof dish. Fry the onion in the pan for 3 to 4 minutes to soften it. Add the sliced carrot and turnip (if used) and continue to fry gently, stirring all the time, for another 3 minutes.

Add the vegetables to the meat in the casserole. Dissolve the bullion cube in 2 cups of boiling water. Sprinkle the flour over the remaining juices in the frying pan and stir. Gradually stir in the stock, stirring hard to make a smooth gravy and adding the salt, pepper, and herbs. Pour the gravy over the meat in the casserole to cover the meat and vegetables.

Then cover the meat with a thick layer of potato slices, placing them so that they overlap and form a thick crust. Dot with butter. Cover with a lid or piece of tight-fitting foil, and cook at 325° for 1½ to 2 hours, removing the lid for the last half-hour of cooking time to brown the top. If the top does not seem to be getting crispy enough, either increase the oven heat to 400° or place the casserole dish under the broiler for a few minutes.

If you have to cook the casserole on top of the stove because an oven is not available, simmer the casserole very gently for 1½ to 2 hours, then brown the potato topping under the broiler as described above.

PORK

It is important that pork be cooked thoroughly; it is better over-cooked than underdone, and must never, ever, be served pink, as rare pork may harbor the dangerous parasite trichinosis. The meat must look pale-colored all the way through.

PORK CHOPS— BROILED OR PAN-FRIED

Quick and easy. Good with sautéed potatoes, broiled or fried tomato, pineapple rings, or a spoonful of apple sauce. Pork is better broiled, since it can be fatty, but frying is quite acceptable if you don't have a broiler. Whichever way you choose to cook it, make sure it is cooked thoroughly. The juices must run clear; not pink, and the meat must be pale-colored all the way through.

Preparation and cooking time: 14–16 minutes.

> 1 pork chop
> A little oil or butter
> ½ tsp. dried mixed herbs (or dried sage)
> 1 tomato (or 1–2 pineapple rings or 1 tbsp. apple
>   sauce)
> Cooked, cold, boiled potatoes to sauté

Heat the broiler or heat a frying pan over a moderate heat with a smear of oil. Rub both sides of the chop with the oil or butter and sprinkle with the herbs. Put the chop either under the hot broiler, turning frequently until brown and crispy, 12 to 15 minutes (lowering the heat if the chop starts getting too brown); or into the hot frying pan, frying over a moderate heat for 12 to 15 minutes and turning frequently until brown and cooked thoroughly.

ACCOMPANIMENTS
Cut the tomato in half, dot with butter and put under the broiler or into the frying pan for the last 3 to 4 minutes of cooking; or put the pineapple slices on top of the chop under the broiler or in the frying pan for 1 to 2 minutes to warm slightly; or prepare the apple sauce in advance from the recipe on page 224 (or use apple sauce from a jar or can from the supermarket). Fry the sautéed potatoes while the chop is cooking (see page 91). If you have only one frying pan, you can cook them in the pan with the chop.

MUSTARD-
GLAZED
PORK CHOP

A tangy hot grilled chop. Serve with new or sautéed potatoes and a green vegetable.

Preparation and cooking time: 17–20 minutes.

> **1 tsp. mustard**
> **1 tsp. brown sugar**
> **1 tsp. butter**
> **1 pork chop**

Heat the broiler. Mix the mustard, sugar, and melted butter together in a cup. Spread this mixture over both sides of the chop. Cook under the hot broiler, turning frequently, until brown and crispy (12 to 15 minutes). Lower the heat if the chop gets too brown too quickly. The pork must be cooked right through.

PORK CHOP
IN BRITISH
CIDER OR
BEER

Absolutely delicious, and the smell of the meal cooking gives you a real appetite.

Preparation and cooking time: 1 hour.

>   1 tsp. cooking oil
>   ½ oz. butter
>   1 large pork chop
>   1 small onion
>   1 small cooking apple (you can use an eating
>   apple if necessary)
>   ⅓–⅔ cup cider or beer
>   Salt and pepper
>   Pinch of dried herbs
>   1 tbsp. cream (you can also use plain yogurt or
>   soured cream)

Heat the oil and butter in a frying pan. Fry both sides of the chop until brown (4 to 5 minutes). Place it in a casserole or an oven-proof dish. Peel and slice the onion, peel and chop the apple, and fry them together in the frying pan, stirring frequently (4 to 5 minutes) until the onion is soft. Add to the meat in the casserole. Pour enough cider or beer into the casserole so that it covers the meat. Add the salt, pepper, and herbs. Cover with a lid or piece of foil and bake at 350° for approximately 45 minutes. (If you don't have an oven, this can be cooked very, very gently in a saucepan on top of the stove for 45 minutes.) Stir in the cream and serve at once.

PORK IN A
PACKET

An easy way of cooking pork, without much cleaning up!

Preparation and cooking time: 1 hour.

> **1–2 tbsp. uncooked long grain rice (or 3 tbsp. cooked rice)**
> **2 tbsp. canned or frozen corn**
> **2 tbsp. frozen peas**
> **1 spring onion (or ½ small onion)**
> **Salt and pepper**
> **Aluminum foil**
> **Butter for greasing the foil**
> **1 pork chop**
> **1 tsp. soy sauce (or Worcestershire sauce)**
> **1 tbsp. cider, white wine, or beer**

Cook the raw rice in boiling, salted water for 8 to 10 minutes until just soft. Add the frozen corn and peas for the last 2 minutes and cook with the rice, or cook by themselves if you are using cooked rice. (Canned corn does not need cooking.)

Drain well. Wash and chop the spring onion or peel and chop the onion. Add the onion to the rice mixture, mix well, and season with salt and pepper.

Cut a square of aluminum foil large enough to wrap the chop loosely. Grease the foil with the butter and put the chop in the center of the foil. Sprinkle with soy or Worcestershire sauce. Top with the rice mixture and moisten with the cider, wine, or beer. Wrap the foil around the chop into a parcel, and put carefully onto a baking tin or dish. Bake at 350° for 40 minutes.

CRUNCHY FRIED PORK

Try to buy thin slices of meat for this dish and flatten them by banging them with a rolling pin. (If you don't have one, use an unopened can wrapped in a plastic bag to pound the slices flat.) A crisp green salad or a fresh tomato can accompany this dish.

Preparation and cooking time: 30 minutes.

> **1–2 potatoes (you can use up cooked potatoes if you have them)**
> **4–6 oz. pork**
> **½ beaten egg (use the rest in scrambled egg)**
> **1 tbsp. dry bread crumbs**
> **1 tbsp. oil (for frying)**
> **1 onion**

Peel the potatoes, cut them in quarters, and cook in boiling salted water for 15 minutes until soft. Flatten the pork as best you can, and if the pieces are large, cut them into portions. Beat the egg. Dip the pork pieces into the egg and then toss them in the dry bread crumbs until thoroughly coated.

Heat the oil in a frying pan. Put the pork pieces carefully into the hot fat and fry both sides of the pork over a medium heat until brown and cooked through (about 15 minutes). Put the pork onto a hot dish and keep warm. Drain the potato when cooked. Cut into cubes. Peel and chop the onion and cook in the fat in the frying pan. Add the cubed potato and continue cooking until just turning brown and crispy, stirring occasionally. Sprinkle the onion and potatoes over the meat and serve hot.

SPARE RIBS

Preparation and cooking time: 1 hour, 30 minutes to 1 hour, 45 minutes.

1 lb. spare ribs
1 small clove garlic (or ¼ tsp. garlic powder)
1 tbsp. soy sauce
1 tsp. orange marmalade
1 small onion
Salt and pepper
½ bullion cube
½ cup boiling water
1 tsp. vinegar

Heat the broiler. Put the ribs in the broiler pan and brown them under the broiler, turning frequently, to seal in the juices. If you don't have a broiler, brown the ribs in a frying pan with a little oil or butter, over a medium heat, for 2 to 3 minutes, turning often. Peel and crush the garlic clove.

Mix the soy sauce, marmalade, and garlic and spread over the ribs. Peel and slice the onion. Put the onion in a casserole or oven-proof dish. Place the ribs on top and season with salt and pepper.

Dissolve the bullion cube in ½ cup of boiling water, add the vinegar and pour it all over the ribs. Cover and cook at 400° for 1½ hours. Remove the lid for the last 20 minutes to allow the meat to become crisp. The sauce should be sticky when cooked. A baked potato can be cooked in the oven with the casserole (see page 92).

PASTA

There are numerous shapes of pasta but they are all cooked in the same way, and most of the different shapes are interchangeable in most recipes, with the exception of the lasagna and cannelloni types.

Spaghetti	— Available in various lengths and thicknesses.
Fancy shapes	— Shells, bows, etc.
Macaroni types	— Thicker tubular shapes.
Lasagna	— Large, flat sheets
Cannelloni	— Usually filled with tasty stuffing.

Most makes of pasta have cooking instructions on the package. *Allow approximately 3 oz. pasta per serving.*

Pasta must be cooked in a large pan of boiling, salted water, with a few drops of cooking oil added to help prevent the pasta from stocking. Long spaghetti is stood in the pan and pushed down gradually as it softens. Let the water come to a boil, then lower the heat and leave to simmer (without the lid, or it will boil over) for 8 to 10 minutes until the past is just cooked (*al dente*). Drain well, preferably in a colander, or you risk losing the pasta down the sink. Serve at once.

MACARONI
AND CHEESE

This is traditionally made with elbow macaroni, but it is equally good with spaghetti or pasta shapes, shells, bows, etc.

Preparation and cooking time: 30 minutes.

> ⅔ cup macaroni or chosen pasta (uncooked)
> **Pinch of salt**
> ½ tsp. cooking oil

For the cheese sauce
> ⅔ cup grated cheese
> **2 tsp. flour**
> ⅔ cup milk
> **1 tbsp. butter**
> **Salt, pepper, and mustard**
> **Tomato (optional)**

For the topping
> ⅓ cup grated cheese

Heat the oven to 400°. Cook the macaroni or pasta in a large saucepan of boiling water with a pinch of salt and a few drops of cooking oil for 8 to 10 minutes, until just cooked (al dente). While the macaroni is cooking, make the cheese sauce: Put the flour in a small bowl and mix it into a paste with a little of the milk. Bring the rest of the milk almost to boiling point in a small pan, then pour it into the flour mixture, stirring all the time. Pour the mixture back into the pan, return to the heat, and bring back to a boil, stirring all the time until the sauce thickens. Beat in the butter, salt, pepper, pinch of mustard, and grated cheese.

Drain the macaroni well and put it into a greased, oven-proof dish. Pour the cheese sauce over the macaroni and mix slightly. Sprinkle the rest of the cheese on top. Put into the hot oven for 10 minutes until the cheese is crisp and bubbling and the macaroni is hot. This dish can be topped with sliced, fresh tomato and served with a salad. The top can be browned under the broiler instead of in the oven, providing the sauce and macaroni are hot when mixed.

BOLOGNESE
SAUCE

This thick, meaty sauce can be used with spaghetti, pasta shapes, lasagne, or even mashed potato (see page 156), for a cheap and cheerful dinner.

Preparation and cooking time: 45 minutes.

Small onion
½ carrot (optional)
½ strip of bacon (optional)
Clove of garlic or pinch of garlic powder
    (optional)
2 tsp. oil or a little grease (for frying)
3-4 oz. ground beef
4 oz. canned tomatoes or 2 fresh tomatoes
2 tsp. tomato purée or tomato ketchup
½ beef bullion cube and ½ cup water or ½ small
    can of tomato soup
Pinch of salt and pepper
Pinch of sugar
Pinch of dried herbs

Peel and chop the onion. Peel and chop or grate the carrot. Chop the bacon. Peel, chop, and crush the garlic clove. Fry the onion and bacon gently in the oil or grease in a saucepan, stirring until the onion is soft (2 to 3 minutes). Add the ground beef and continue cooking, stirring until it is lightly browned. Add the carrot, canned tomatoes (or chopped fresh ones), tomato purée (or ketchup), bullion cube, and water (or the soup), stirring well. Add the salt, pepper, sugar, and herbs. Bring to a boil, then lower the heat and simmer, stirring occasionally, for 20 to 30 minutes, until the meat is tender.

SPAGHETTI
BOLOGNESE

Preparation and cooking time: 25–55 minutes.

Bolognese sauce (see page 203)
3 oz. spaghetti or 1 cup pasta shells, bows, etc.
½ tsp. cooking oil
2 tsp. Parmesan cheese

Prepare the Bolognese sauce. Cook the spaghetti or chosen pasta in a pan of boiling, salted water with ½ tsp. cooking oil for 8 to 10 minutes. (If you want to have long spaghetti, stand the bundle of spaghetti in the boiling water and, as it softens, coil it round into the water without breaking.) Drain the spaghetti and put it onto a hot plate. Pour the sauce into the center of the spaghetti and sprinkle the cheese on top. Serve at once.

SPAGHETTI
PORK
SAVORY

Preparation and cooking time: 30 minutes.

> **3 oz. pasta—spaghetti, shells, noodles, etc.**
> **A little cooking oil**
> **2 oz. pork**
> **1 onion**
> **2 fresh tomatoes or 1 8 oz. can tomatoes**
> **⅓ cup grated cheddar cheese, or a little Parmesan**

Cook the pasta in a large saucepan of boiling, salted water, with a few drops of cooking oil, for 8 to 10 minutes (see page 199). Drain and keep hot. Meanwhile, cut the pork into tiny strips, discarding fat and gristle. Peel and chop the onions and chop the fresh tomatoes (if used). Heat some oil in a frying pan. Add the onion and sauté for a few minutes to soften it. Add the pork strips and sauté, stirring well, until browned. Add the tomato pieces or canned tomatoes (without the juice) and stir well.

Cook over a low heat for another 10 minutes, stirring to break up the tomatoes, until you have a thick sauce. Pour the hot sauce over the spaghetti, and serve at once, sprinkled with the grated cheese.

QUICK
LASAGNA

For this recipe you can use Bolognese sauce (page 203) or a commercially prepared spaghetti sauce.

Preparation and cooking time: 25–30 minutes.

> **3–4** sheets lasagna noodles
> **5 oz.** condensed chicken (or mushroom) soup
>   mixed with ¼ can milk or water
> **⅓ cup** grated cheese

Put the Bolognese sauce in a pan and heat gently for 3 to 5 minutes, stirring well, to make a thin sauce (add a little water if needed). Grease an oven-proof dish—the square aluminum pans are excellent for one portion. Put layers of the meat sauce, lasagne noodles, and soup in the dish, ending with a layer of soup. Make sure the lasagne is completely covered with the sauce. Top with the grated or thinly-sliced cheese. Bake for 15 to 20 minutes at 375° until the cheese is golden and bubbling. This dish can be served with a green salad.

CHEESY
NOODLES

A cheap dish for using up the contents of the cupboard or refrigerator.

Preparation and cooking time: 15 minutes.

> **3 oz. uncooked noodles**
> **1 tsp. oil**
> **⅔ cup grated cheese**
> **2 tbsp. butter**
> **Salt and pepper**

Cook the noodles in a large saucepan of boiling, salted water with 1 tsp. cooking oil until just soft (about 7 to 10 minutes). Drain the noodles, return to the hot, dry pan, and shake for a moment in the pan over the heat to dry them and keep them hot. Remove from the heat and stir in the cheese and the butter. Season with salt and pepper and pile onto a hot dish. Serve at once with tomato or a salad.

"SUNDAY LUNCH" DISHES

This chapter shows simply and clearly how to cook a Sunday lunch: how to roast beef, chicken, lamb and pork. There are also recipes at the end of the chapter on how to make gravy and the other different sauces that accompany the various meats. All the "Sunday Lunch" recipes are for several people—according to the size of roast you buy. Useful when you have weekend visitors.

ROAST BEEF

It is best if several people can share a roast, since a very small roast tends to shrink up during cooking.

Roasts to choose for roasting:

> Sirloin tip, eye of round, or rolled rump.
> Standing or rolled rib—most tender.

Choose a roast of beef that looks appetizing, with clear, bright, red, lean meat and firm, pale-cream fat. A good roast must have a little fat with it or it will be too dry when cooked.

Make sure you know the weight of the roast you buy, because cooking time depends on the weight. *You should allow approximately 6 oz. uncooked weight of beef per person*, so a roast weighing 2½–3 lb. should provide 6 to 8 helpings. (Remember, you can save some cold meat for leftovers next day.)

For underdone "rare," beef allow 15 minutes per pound plus an extra 15 minutes. For medium-rare beef allow 20 minutes per pound plus an extra 20 minutes. Remember that a small roast will cook through quicker, so allow slightly less time.

Serve beef with Yorkshire pudding (see page 212), horseradish sauce, gravy (see page 220), roast potatoes (see page 89) and assorted vegetables or a green salad.

Place the roast in a greased roasting pan. The roast, or the whole pan, may be covered with foil to help keep the meat moist, but need not be. Roast at 400° for the appropriate time (as explained above). Test that the meat is cooked by stabbing it with a fork or vegetable knife and noting the color of the juices that run out: the redder the juice, the rarer the meat. When the meat is cooked, lift it our carefully onto a hot plate and make the gravy (see page 220).

For the potatoes: calculate when he roast will be ready and allow the potatoes 45 to 60 min tes oasting time, according to size. They can be roasted around the meat or in a separate pan in the oven.

YORKSHIRE
PUDDING

Individual Yorkshire puddings are baked in muffin tins, but a larger pudding can be cooked in any baking pan (not one with a loose base). They do not cook well in a Pyrex-type dish.

Preparation and cooking time: 25 minutes (small), 40–45 minutes (large).

> 4 heaped tbsp. plain flour
> A pinch of salt
> 1 egg
> 1⅓ cups milk
> A little oil or fat

Put the flour and salt in a large bowl. Add the egg and beat into the flour, gradually adding the milk and beating to make a smooth batter. (The easiest way of doing this is with a hand or electric mixer, but with a bit more effort you get just as good a result using a whisk, a wooden spoon, or even a fork.) Beat well.

Grease the tines and place on the top shelf of a 400° oven for a few minutes to get hot. Give the batter a final whisk and pour it into the tins. Bake until firm and golden brown. Try not to open the oven door for the first 10 minutes so that the puddings rise well. If you want meat and puddings ready together, start cooking the puddings 25 minutes before the meat is ready for small puddings, 40-45 minutes before for large puddings.

ROAST
CHICKEN

Before cooking a previously frozen chicken, make sure it is completely defrosted. It can be soaked in cold water to get rid of the last bits of ice and hurry the thawing process, but do not try to thaw it in hot water, and do not thaw at room temperature.

A 4–5 lb. chicken will serve 4 to 6 people, according to appetite. Make sure you know the weight of the bird, because cooking time depends on the weight.

Allow 20 minutes per pound plus 20 minutes extra, if the chicken is stuffed.

Chicken is traditionally served with thyme and parsley stuffing (see page 226). We like apple sauce (see page 224) or cranberry sauce with it as well. Roast potatoes, parsnips, carrots, and brussels sprouts are tasty with chicken in the winter, while new potatoes and peas make a good summer dinner (see the vegetable section page 59).

> **1 chicken (completely defrosted)**
> **Oil and butter (for roasting)**
> **Cooking foil**

Heat the oven to 400°. Rinse the chicken in cold water and dry with paper towels.

Spread the butter and oil liberally over the chicken and either wrap loosely in foil and put it into a pan or place in a greased roasting pan and cover the pan with foil. Put the chicken in the pan into the hot oven. Calculate the cooking time so that the rest of the dinner is ready at the same time.

Roast potatoes (see page 89) and parsnips (see page 84) can be cooked around the chicken or in a separate roasting pan. Allow about 45 to 60 minutes cooking time.

Remove or open the foil for the last 15 minutes of cooking time to brown the chicken. Test that the chicken is cooked by prodding it with a pointed knife or fork in the thickest part, inside the thigh. The juices should run clear; if they are still pink, cook for a little longer. Remove the chicken carefully onto a hot plate and use the juices in the pan to make the gravy (see page 220).

ROAST LEG
OR SHOULDER
OF LAMB

Choose between leg and shoulder roasts. Shoulder tends to be more fatty. These roasts are usually sold on the bone, so you have to allow more weight or meat for each person than you do with beef. However, trying to carve a shoulder of lamb can provide quite an entertaining cabaret act! *Allow at least 8 oz. per serving.*

You don't have to buy a whole leg or shoulder; half legs and shoulders, or a piece of a very large roast can be bought. Make sure you know the weight of the meat you buy, because cooking time depends on the weight.

The traditional accompaniments for lamb are:

    mint sauce (see page 225)

    mint jelly, red currant jelly, or onion sauce (see page 222).

Serve with roast potatoes (see page 89), parsnips (see page 84) or other vegetables.

Allow 20 minutes per pound plus an extra 20 minutes.

Leg or shoulder of lamb

Oil or dripping (for roasting)

2–3 garlic cloves (optional)

2–3 sprigs rosemary (optional)

The preparation of this dish may seem a little more involved than that of some others in this book, but it is worth the effort.

Heat the oven to 400°. Place the roast in a roasting pan with a little oil or dripping. If you like the flavor of garlic, you can insert 1 or 2 peeled cloves under the skin of the meat, near the bone, but this is not really necessary. Rosemary sprigs can be used in the same way.

Cover the roast, or the whole pan with aluminum foil. (This helps to keep the meat from shriveling up.) Roast it in the hot oven for the calculated time (20 minutes per pound plus an extra 20 minutes), removing the foil for the last 20 to 30 minutes of the cooking time to brown the meat, if pale. Roast potatoes and parsnips can be cooked with the roast for the last hour of cooking.

Test that the lamb is cooked at the end of the cooking time by stabbing it with a fork or vegetable knife. Lamb is traditionally served pink in the middle, but many people prefer it cooked more; it is entirely a matter of personal preference. The meat juices should run slightly pink for underdone lamb and clear when the lamb is better cooked.

When the meat is cooked satisfactorily, lift it carefully

onto a hot plate and make the gravy (see page 220). Serve with mint sauce (see page 225).

ROAST
PORK

Most pork roasts are sold with the bone in, so you have to allow more weight of meat per serving. It also makes it more difficult to carve.

Roasts to choose from:
    Leg
    Shoulder
    Loin (left in one piece, not cut up into chops)

Allow approximately 8 oz. per serving. Make sure you know the weight of the roast you buy, because cooking time depends on the weight.

Allow 25 minutes per pound cooking time plus 25 minutes extra.

Pork is traditionally served with sage and onion stuffing (see page 226), and apple sauce (see page 224). Also serve it with roast potatoes (see page 89) and parsnips (see page 84) or other vegetables.

Heat the oven to 400° so that the roast goes into a hot oven, to make the crackling crisp. Rub the pork skin with oil and sprinkle with salt to give the crackling a good flavor. Place the roast in the roasting pan with a little oil or grease to keep it from sticking to the pan. Put the pan into the hot oven and calculate the cooking time so that the rest of the dinner can be ready at the right time.

After 20 minutes or so, when the crackling is looking

crisp, the roast or the whole pan can be covered with foil to keep the meat from getting too brown (smaller roasts will brown more easily). Roast potatoes or parsnips can be cooked around the meat for the last hour of the cooking time, or in a separate roasting pan (see page 89 or 84).

Test that the meat is cooked at the end of the cooking time: the juices should run either clear when prodded with a knife or fork. If they are still pink, cook for a bit longer. Pork must be cooked through (it is better overcooked than under-done) as rare pork can cause food poisoning. The meat should be pale-colored, not pink. When the meat is completely cooked, lift the roast onto a hot plate and make the gravy (see next page).

GRAVY

Often the meat juices alone from grilled or fried meat make a tasty sauce poured over the meat. But if you want to make "real" gravy remember that the more flour you use, the thicker the gravy. The liquid can be any mixture of water, vegetable water, wine, sherry or beer.

Preparation and cooking time: 4 minutes.

> **1–2 tsp. cornflour or flour and 1 tsp. gravy flavoring powder**
> **1 cup water or vegetable water and/or wine, beer or sherry**
> **Any juices from the meat**

Mix the cornflour or flour and the gravy flavoring powder (if used) into a smooth paste with a little of the cold water, wine, sherry, or beer (depending on what you're drinking). Add the rest of the water and the meat juices from the roasting tin. Pour the mixture into a small saucepan, and bring to the boil, stirring all the time. Add more liquid if the gravy is too thick, or more flour mixture if it is too thin.

To thicken the gravy used in stews and casseroles, make the gravy mixture as above. Stir the mixture into the stew or casserole and bring to the boil so that the gravy can thicken as it cooks.

WHITE
SAUCE

This is a quick way to make a basic sauce, to which you can add other ingredients or flavorings.

Preparation and cooking time: 5 minutes.

> **1 tbsp. flour**
> **1 cup milk**
> **1 tbsp. butter (or margarine)**
> **Salt and pepper**

Put the flour in a large cup or small bowl. Mix it into a tin paste with 1 tbsp. of the milk. Heat the rest of the milk in a saucepan, but do not boil. Pour it into the well-stirred flour mixture, stirring all the time. Pour the mixture back into the saucepan, return to the heat, and bring to a boil, stirring all the time, until the sauce thickens. Beat in the butter or margarine. Season with the salt and pepper.

CHEESE SAUCE
Grate ⅓–⅔ cup cheese. Add to the white sauce with the butter and add a dash of mustard if you have any.

PARSLEY SAUCE
Wash and drain a handful of sprigs of parsley. Chop they finely with a knife or scissors, and add to the sauce with the salt or pepper.

ONION
SAUCE

A quick and easy method. Onion sauce is traditionally served with lamb, and is also tasty poured over cauliflower.

Preparation and cooking time: 25 minutes.

> **1 onion**
> **1 cup water**
> **1 tbsp. flour**
> **1 cup milk**
> **1 tbsp. butter**
> **Salt and pepper**

Peel and finely chop the onion. Put it into a small saucepan with the cup of water. Bring to a boil, then lower the heat and cook gently for 10 to 15 minutes until the onion is soft. In a bowl, mix the flour into a paste with a little of the milk. Gradually add this to the onion mixture, stirring all the time as the mixture thickens. Add more milk, until the sauce is just thick enough. Beat in the butter, and season with the salt and pepper. Serve hot.

"INSTANT"
SAUCE MIX

Several makes of sauce mix are now widely available at supermarkets. Follow the instructions on the packet, and only make up as much sauce as is needed for the recipe. Keep the rest of the packet for later, tightly closed, in a dry cupboard or refrigerator.

APPLE
SAUCE

You can buy jars or cans of apple purée, but it is nicer and very easy to make your own. Apple sauce is served with roast pork or poultry.

Preparation and cooking time: 10–15 minutes.

> **1–2 cooking apple**
> **2–3 tbsp. water**
> **1–2 tbsp. sugar**

Peel, core and slice the apples. Put them in a saucepan with the water and bring to the boil gently. Simmer for 5 to 10 minutes until the apples are soft (do not let them boil dry). Add the sugar to taste (be careful, the apples will be *very* hot) and mash with a fork until smooth.

MINT SAUCE

You can buy jars of mint sauce at the supermarket, but I think they taste better if you re-mix the sauce with a little sugar and 1 to 2 teaspoons of fresh vinegar. Mint sauce is traditionally served with lamb.

"BOUGHT" MINT SAUCE

> **3–4 tsp. "bought" mint sauce**
> **1 tsp. granulated sugar**
> **1–2 tsp. vinegar**

Mix all the above ingredients together in a small glass or dish.

"FRESH" MINT SAUCE

> **Handful of fresh mint sprigs**
> **2–3 tbsp. vinegar (wine vinegar if you have it)**
> **1–2 tsp. granulated sugar**

Strip the leaves from the stems. Wash well, drain and chop the mint as finely as possible. Mix the mint, vinegar and sugar in a small glass or dish, and serve with the lamb. This sauce will keep in a small, covered jar in the refrigerator.

STUFFING

Traditionally, sage and onion flavored stuffing goes with pork, while thyme and parsley goes with chicken, but any mixture of herbs is tasty.

Preparation and cooking time: 35–45 minutes.

> **1 small package (3 oz.) stuffing**
> **A little butter or margarine**
> **Hot water—you can use water from the kettle or**
> **vegetable water**

Make up the stuffing according to the directions on the packet. Grease an oven-proof dish, put the stuffing into the dish, dot with the butter. Bake in the oven at 400° with the roast for 30 to 40 minutes, until crispy on top.

CAKES AND DESSERTS

A few easy recipes for those with a sweet tooth. Of course, delicious chilled and frozen deserts, gooey cakes and other treats are widely available ready-made in stores. You can also choose among countless cake, pudding, and cookie mixes on the supermarket shelves. With the addition of butter and eggs you can easily produce a home-made cake.

QUICK CHOCOLATE SAUCE—FOR ICE CREAM

Fast, easy, and most effective. Chocolaty but not too rich.

Preparation and cooking time: 5 minutes.

> **1–2 oz. sweetened chocolate (such as a Hershey's candy bar)**
> **1 tsp. cold water**

Break the chocolate into a ceramic or Pyrex bowl and add the water. Stand the bowl in 1 inch of hot water in a saucepan over a low heat and simmer gently until the chocolate melts. Stir well, and pour over scoops of ice cream.

HOT
CHOCOLATE
SAUCE

A rich, fudgy sauce, that's delicious with vanilla, chocolate or coffee ice cream.

Preparation and cooking time: 10 minutes.

> **2 oz. chocolate chips, chocolate icing, or a chocolate bar**
> **1 tbsp. brown sugar**
> **1 tbsp. cold water**
> **2 tbsp. butter (unsalted is best)**
> **2 tsp. rum (optional)**

Put the chocolate, sugar, and water into a small saucepan over a low heat and stir until the chocolate melts and the mixture is smooth and creamy. Remove from the heat. Add the butter in small flakes. Beat well. Beat in the rum, if used. Serve over scoops of ice cream. If necessary, re-heat the sauce later by putting it into a Pyrex or ceramic basin and following the directions for Quick Chocolate sauce, on preceding page.

BANANA
SPLIT

Full of calories, but absolutely delicious!

Preparation time: 5 minutes (plus the time for making the chocolate sauce).

> 1 large banana
> Ice cream
> Chocolate sauce (bought or home-made—see
>   page 229)
> Whipped cream
> Chopped nuts (for decoration—optional)
> Chocolate sprinkles (for decoration—optional)

Split the banana in half, lengthways and place halves in a dish with two or three scoops of ice cream between them. Spoon the chocolate sauce over the top. Decorate with the whipped cream and sprinkle nuts or chocolate sprinkles on the top. Eat immediately.

FRUIT
PAVLOVA

Delicious in the summertime! Make it with cream, ice cream—or both!

Preparation time: 5 minutes.

> 1–2 tbsp. fresh or canned fruit—raspberries, strawberries, canned peaches, tangerines, pineapples, or pears
> Cream, whipped cream, and/or ice cream
> 1–2 meringue nests (available from supermarkets)

Prepare this dish just before you are ready to eat it. Wash and drain the fresh fruit, or drain the canned fruit. Spread the cream or ice cream over the meringue nests. Arrange the fruit carefully on top of the cream or ice cream. Decorate with a spoonful of whipped cream. Serve at once.

LEMON
MERINGUE
(PIE)

This can be made with or without pastry. You will need a whisk or electric mixer to make the meringue.

Preparation and cooking time: 20 minutes (for soft meringue), 35 minutes (for crisp meringue). This will make 2–3 servings.

> **1 egg**
> **1 10 oz. box lemon home pie mix**
> **1¼ cups cold water**
> **1 tbsp. lemon juice (optional)**
> **1 tbsp. sugar (optional**
> **7-in. diameter pastry shell (optional—available**
>   **from supermarkets)**
> **2 heaped tbsp. sugar**

Heat the oven to 400° for soft meringue or 325° for crisp meringue. Separate the egg (see page 39). It is important that you separate the egg completely, since otherwise the meringue will not beat properly. Prepare the lemon pie mix with the water, following the instructions on the package. Stir it well over a low heat so that the mixture doesn't burn. Stir in the lemon juice and extra tablespoon of sugar according to taste. Pour this filling into either a 7-inch oven-proof dish or the pastry shell (place this on a baking pan before filling).

If necessary, remove any traces of yolk from the egg

white with a metal spoon, then make the meringue by beating the egg white hard with a whisk or electric mixer until it is very stiff, thick, and foamy and will form snowy peaks. Add the 2 heaped tbsp. of sugar, one teaspoonful at a time, beating well until all the sugar is added. The mixture should still be very thick and stiff. Spoon the meringue over the lemon filling, covering it completely and sealing it in well at the edges.

Lightly brown in the oven, for 5 minutes in the hot oven for a soft meringue or 20 minutes in the cooler oven for a crisp meringue (this one keeps better if you're not going to eat it at once). Keep an eye on the meringue while it is in the oven to make sure it does not get too brown. Serve hot or cold.

CRÊPES

These can be sweet or savory and are delicious at any time. Sweet crêpes are traditionally served sprinkled with a tsp. of sugar and a squeeze of lemon. For sweet and savory fillings, see page 32. *This recipe makes 6 to 8 pancakes.*

Preparation time: 10 minutes (plus 1 minute per crêpe cooking time).

> **4 heaped tbsp. plain flour**
> **1 egg**
> **1¼ cups milk**
> **Oil for frying—not butter**

Prepare the filling, if used. Put the flour into a bowl, add the egg, and beat it into the flour. Gradually add the milk and beat to make a smooth batter. (The easiest way of doing this is with a hand or electric mixer, but with a bit of effort you get just as good a result using a wooden spoon or even a fork.)

Heat a clean frying pan over a moderate heat, and when hot but not burning, grease the pan lightly with oil. Pour in a little batter, enough to cover the pan thinly. Tilt the pan to spread the batter over it. Fry briskly until just set on top and lightly browned underneath, shaking the pan occasionally to keep the crêpe from sticking; this will only take a few moments.

Toss the crêpe or flip it over with a knife and fry for a few more moments to cook the other side. Turn it out onto a warm plate. Sprinkle with lemon and sugar, or add the filling, and roll up or fold into four.

Crêpes taste best eaten at once, straight from the pan, but

they can be filled, rolled up and kept warm while you cook the rest. Wipe the pan with a paper towel, re-heat and re-grease it and cook the next crêpe at before.

GRILLED
PEACHES

Absolutely delicious with fresh peaches, but very good with canned fruit, too. Buy cheap peaches in the summer for a treat. Serve with cream or ice cream.

Preparation and cooking time: 5 minutes.

> **1–2 fresh peaches or 1 cup of canned peaches**
> **1 tbsp. butter**
> **2 tbsp. brown sugar**

Peel and slice the fresh peaches or drain and slice the canned peaches. Butter an oven-proof dish and place the peach slices in it. Sprinkle thickly with the brown sugar, dot with butter. Place the dish under a hot broiler for a minute or two so that the sugar melts and the peach slices warm through. Serve at once with cream or ice cream, if liked.

PEACHES
WITH SYRUP

Make this delicious dessert in the summer when peaches are in season. Serve with cream or ice cream. (This dish can be prepared, but not cooked, in advance, the cold fruit being left to soak in the syrup and then put in the oven to cook while you are eating dinner.)

Preparation and cooking time: 15 minutes.

> **2 tbsp. brown sugar**
> **⅓ cup water**
> **1–2 peaches**

Preheat oven to 350°. Make the syrup: put the brown sugar and water into a small saucepan and bring to a boil, stirring occasionally. Simmer gently for 3 to 4 minutes to dissolve the sugar. Wash the peaches (do not peel) and cut them in half, from top to bottom. Remove the pits. Put the peaches into an oven-proof dish with the cut sides face upward and pour the hot syrup over them, spooning it into the holes left by the pits. Bake for 10 to 15 minutes until the fruit is hot and the syrup bubbling. Serve hot with lots of cream or ice cream.

LIQUEUR ORANGES— FOR 2

Delicious, simple, and rather unusual, so save it for when you are entertaining a special friend.

Preparation time: 5 minutes. Chilling time: 1–2 hours, but longer if possible; all day is best.

> **2 large, sweet oranges**
> **2 tbsp. sugar**
> **1 tbsp. orange liqueur—Cointreau, Grand**
>   **Marnier, or Curaçao (you can buy a**
>   **miniature bottle of liqueur)**
> **Whipped cream (optional)**

Peel the oranges and scrape away any of the white inner peel remaining. Cut the oranges into thin rings and arrange the slices in a shallow serving dish. Sprinkle with the sugar and liqueur. Cover the dish with a plate or plastic wrap and leave it in the refrigerator or in a cold place for at least an hour, but all day if possible, to chill and let the liqueur soak in. Serve alone or with whipped cream.

CHOCOLATE
CRUNCHIES

This has to be one of the easiest dessert recipes there is, anywhere.

Preparation and cooking time: 5 minutes.

> **4 oz. chocolate icing, sweetened cooking
> chocolate, or chocolate bar
> 1¼ cups cornflakes or rice crispies
> 12–15 paper baking cups**

Break the chocolate into a Pyrex or ceramic bowl. Stand this in 1 inch of hot water in a saucepan and simmer over a gentle heat until the chocolate melts. Remove the bowl from the heat, stir in the cornflakes or rice crispies, and mix until they are well-coated with the chocolate. Spoon into the paper baking cups and leave to set. Store in a cookie tin or plastic box.

CHOCOLATE
KRISPIES

Almost everyone likes these, and they're cheap too.

Preparation and cooking time: 15 minutes.

> 4 tbsp. butter or margarine
> 2 tbsp. sugar
> 2 tbsp. light corn syrup
> 2 tbsp. unsweetened cocoa powder
> 2 cups cornflakes or rice crispies
> 12–15 paper baking cups
> (instead of the sugar and cocoa powder you can
> use 4 tbsp. sweetened cocoa powder)

Put the butter (or margarine), sugar, and corn syrup in a medium-sized saucepan and heat over a gentle heat until melted. Add the cocoa and stir well until you have a chocolate syrup. Stir in the cornflakes or rice crispies and mix well to coat them thoroughly with the chocolate. Heap them into paper baking cups and leave to set. Store in a cookie tin or plastic container.